SKIPPING DOWN MEMORY LANE

by

Joyce Rapier

Edited by Vaughanda Bowie

TigerEye Publications
P.O. Box 6382
Springdale, AR 72766
www.TigerEyePubs.com

SKIPPING DOWN MEMORY LANE
Copyright © 2011 by Joyce Rapier

All rights reserved. No part of this book may be reproduced or transmitted in any form or by any means without written permission from the author.

© 2011: TXu 1-756-950

ISBN: 146803541X

Printed in USA

Dedication

To my husband, Dan, who supports me with my writing endeavors and to my children and friends whose memories fill my heart with warmth.

Special Thanks:

Mahesh Grossman

Author Mahesh Grossman is a ghostwriter, publisher and editor of more than 60 books. His works include "*Write a Book Without Lifting a Finger: How to Hire a Ghostwriter even if You're on a Shoestring Budget*" and "*The Silly Rubber Band Handbook.*" He is also co-author, as Steven M. Grossman, of "*Color Your Hair Like a Pro.*" He has been on more than 100 TV and radio shows including Fox and Friends and was written about in more than a dozen papers, including USA Today and the Los Angeles Times. His expertise garnered him speaker on "*How to Book More Business by Becoming an Author.*" Grossman also quarterbacked the Black Republican Salute to Richard Nixon, an event that was covered by Newsweek and brought the former president back to the public eye after years of seclusion. He is president of the Authors Team (www.AuthorsTeam.com) and 10 Finger Press.

Susan Reynolds

Susan Reynolds is the creator and editor of Adams Media's *My Hero* series, which includes *My Teacher Is My Hero* (2008), *My Mom Is My Hero* (2009), *My Dad Is My Hero* (2009), and *My Dog Is My Hero* (2010). She also edited *Woodstock Revisited*, 50 far out, groovy, peace-inducing, flashback-inducing stories from those who were there. Ms. Reynolds owns Literary Cottage, a literary consulting firm based in Boston, through which she coaches other writers in pursuit of happiness through publishing.

Dahlynn & Ken McKowen

Together, Dahlynn and Ken McKowen have nearly 60 years of professional writing, editing, publication, marketing and public relations experience. Full-time authors and travel writers, when they reached more than 2,000 articles, stories, and photographs published, they stopped counting!

A writing highlight has been as coauthors and consultants for the famed *Chicken Soup for the Soul* series, where they collaborated with founders Jack Canfield and Mark Victor Hansen for more than a decade. Royalty-based books include *Chicken Soup for the Entrepreneur's Soul; Chicken Soup for the Soul in Menopause; Chicken Soup for the Fisherman's Soul*; and *Chicken Soup for the Soul: Celebrating Brothers and Sisters.* They have also edited and ghost-created many more books for this company.

Another facet of the couple's writing career is working one-on-one with the nation's top entrepreneurs and CEOs, providing ghostwriting and editing services. Their integrity and reputation is such that they have ghostwritten for a former President, more than two dozen Fortune 100 and 500 founders and a few California governors. And Dahlynn sits on the induction committee for the EPIcenter: International Entrepreneur Hall of Fame in Atlanta, Georgia, where she will help shape this organization and assist in fundraising for its new state-of-the-art building and entrepreneur-driven educational facility.

On the travel side, the McKowens have written the national award-winner *Best of California's Missions, Mansions and Museums,* as well as *Best of Oregon and Washington's Mansions, Museums and More* and *The Wine-Oh! Guide to California's Sierra Foothills,* all for acclaimed outdoor publisher Wilderness Press.

Under their own publishing house—Publishing Syndicate—the McKowens are creating several new book and anthology series with noted authors. And wanting to continue the success of their wine books, the McKowens will release the *Wine Wherever* series under their own publishing house. If that's not enough, they are also the creators of 13 iPhone winery-destination journaling apps under the *Wine Wherever* brand.

To learn more about the McKowens, please visit www.PublishingSyndicate.com.

CONTENTS

1. Typewriters (15)
2. Halloween Scavenger Hunt (19)
3. The Legend of Sleepy Hollow (23)
4. Sassafras Tea (27)
5. Black & White Television (31)
6. Quiet (35)
7. Long Bell Methodist Episcopal Church, South (39)
8. Bats, Irish Jigs & Turnip Greens (43)
9. Jolt from Jalapeño Peppers (47)
10. Worldburger, Grandburger & Tamales (51)
11. The Big Giant (55)
12. City Park & Activities (59)
13. Crawford County Genealogical Society, Inc. (63)

14. Private Telephone Conversations (67)

15. In Sourcing vs. Out Sourcing (71)

16. Kites & March Wind (75)

17. Blue Law (79)

18. The Old Two Lane Bridge (83)

19. Lost and Found (86)

20. Snipe Hunting (90)

21. Antlion & Doodlebug (94)

22. Fishin' & Giggin' (98)

23. Give Me a Live Body (102)

24. I Am Not Ellie Mae Clampett (106)

25. You'll Be Sorrrr-REEEE! (110)

26. An Era Gone Dim (114)

27. Arthur Stop! (118)

28. Chug, Chug, Chug (122)

29. Addicted to Crunch Kernels (126)

30. Go Carts (130)

31. The Love in Grandma's Hands (134)

32. Halloween Haunted House (138)

33. In the Wild (143)

34. Little Things Mean a Lot (147)

35. Melt Them Down (152)

36. October Morn (156)

37. Old Forecasting (159)

38. Parades (162)

39. Fruit Fights (166)

40. Red-Eye Gravy (170)

41. Romance of the Rails (173)

42. Virtual Reality Sitcom (178)

43. Porch Swings (182)

44. Take Me Out to the Ballgame (186)

45. Tis – Tain't (190)

46. Twin City Bus (194)

47. Washing Machines
 & Old Fashion Candy (199)

48. Who Would'a Thunk It (203)

49. Will Rogers (207)

50. Heroes and Christmas (211)

51. Connect the Dots (215)

52. Do You See What I See (218)

53. E.T. Phone Home (223)

54. Seven Wonders (227)

55. Caves (231)

56. Monkey See Monkey Do (235)

57. Lye Soap (239)

58. Gloom & Doom (243)

59. Tent Revivals (246)

60. Mother's Day – Red or White (250)

61. Four-Way Test (254)

62. Brownies (258)

Epilogue (262)

Preface

These stories are a continuation from my first book, *A Picture Frame of Memories.* As most of you know, since 2009 I have been writing a weekly guest column for the *Press Argus-Courier.* The first story began when I read about the passing of Mrs. Bates, one of the kindest people ever to cross my path. I had no idea people would phone me and reminisce about the things I mentioned. One thing that never crossed my mind is that Kenneth Fry; Editor of the *Press Argus-Courier,* would phone and tell me I wrote myself into a job. Job? It's not a job, it's something I enjoy. Sometimes stories flow like a gentle creek and other times, well, the raging river consumes me.

Like Mrs. Bates, many people have touched me. We never know when someone will enter our sphere of life as the world turns in various directions. It could be through a smile, encouraging words or gentle compassion. We all travel through the same orbit but while on our journey to complete life, paths cross and engulf us. For all the people, large and small, old and young, you have given me the greatest gift. It's the memories I treasure. Some enter my mind as a soft ball of cotton begging to be touched and others erupt without warning.

We've all been through triumphs, sadness, fear and joy and watched as those near us are hurt in some tragic occurrence. Each one of these things bear memories but it's how we manage our lives that get us through trying times. We try to suffocate some memories as they are painful but to live through them helps give us strength. I have had my fair share of those types of memories but as I reflect on them, they are nothing but a stepping stone…a small speed bump designed to keep me in check. For all memories I try to live this quote, one that I created. "Happiness is the road to success, success leads to rewards, rewards are smiles and smiles are crown jewels."

As you read these stories in my book, *Skipping Down Memory Lane*, I hope you remember your own memories, good and bad. They are with us for a reason. All I ask of you is to write down what you remember and share those memories with your families. They are treasures of the heart, mind, soul and body. So, for a little while, come skip with me.

SKIPPING DOWN MEMORY LANE
Book II

By:

Joyce Rapier

JOYCE RAPIER

Skipping Down Memory Lane

Autograph Page

To my wonderful sister!

I love you so much and remember great things — Even some rotten things I did — Shudder!

Hope you enjoy my ramblings.

Your sis,
Joyce

Skipping Down Memory Lane

JOYCE RAPIER

TYPEWRITERS

For the last several days I have been on a merry-go-round, turned Ferris wheel with my computer. Around in circles, gitty-up-go, those carnival horses made me sick to my stomach and it was more than I could tolerate. I was turning a ghastly shade of puke blue. Then…up one day and down the next on the Ferris wheel, I ultimately got stuck at the top with nowhere to go. I hate heights and get vertigo standing on a ladder. Imagine what I felt like on the top of a swinging Ferris wheel.

Hanging in midair, it's as though the world turned me into a blithering state of confusion and zapped me bonkers. I was confused and it's not one of my better traits. To think I have become so entrenched in computerism idiocy is beyond comprehension. Never in my wildest dreams did I think a computer, invented by mere man, would grab me by the hair of the head and fling me into oblivion. I was up to my eyeballs in a spittering and sputtering bloody fight with an inanimate object.

At some point in time, I thought, if I had a cannon with a fifty pound shot, there would have been a hole the size of downtown Van Buren in my house. The computer would have been pulverized. In order to maintain sanity in thinking my book's folder was not circling in cyberspace, Dan calmly pulled out the back-up and handed it to me. It was so beautiful, I kissed it. It was in my hands safe and sound. The books I have written, the current one due for publication in March 2010 and stories published with the Press Argus - Courier and Chicken Soup for the Soul clamored for my attention. All my thoughts pecked away on a keyboard were not destroyed. Although I lost email accounts and favorites, my important business and general documents were spared. I have to admit, though, without a computer it's amazing the kind of work a person can do. I didn't want to clean closets as it's a job for winter so the house and yard garnered my attention. Still, my mind was running amok with stories needing to be written so a note pad caught various titles. Sure, I still know how to do longhand but the keyboard is so handy.

It brought to mind high school typing "commercial" class and how it seemed to overwhelm my fingertips. Gargantuan black manual typewriters sat on desktops and the keyboard seemed stair stepped. While some students took to the Underwood typewriter as a fish to water, I could not make my left hand understand what my right hand was doing. It was a battle royal. The old saying goes, "A person is not in their right mind" held true for me. Since I am right handed, the left side of my brain controlled my way of thinking and manual dexterity. The only person in the "right mind" is the left handed person.

Our lovely petite teacher was extraordinarily adept with her expertise. Gingerly, she took my hands and placed them correctly on the keys. After a few sessions in learning how to approach and angle the hands, I began to type. However, there was one little obstacle. The return was not one of the easiest things to do, especially when you whack it so hard it flies off the typewriter. I am not sure how it happened but to this day, I can see the roller come unhinged and flail through the air.

A part of the black gooey ribbon whizzed overhead while the remainder lodged beneath one of the keys. It was a mess. I had black inky gunk all over my clothes and on my face. If the classroom had been facing the north, instead of the south, the return gizmo would have crashed through the north side window. Thank goodness the bell rang when it did or I would have been the one to clean up the misguided missile. Unfortunately, cleaning up my face and hands was the hard part. There was only pink colored, stinky hand soap in the girl's room and I managed to make everything worse. Ink was on the lavatory, on the old crank handle of the paper (sandpaper towel) dispenser and splattered on my blouse. At the time I was in the restroom, if I had remembered the water flowed out of the faucet with the force of a fire hydrant, it wouldn't have been so bad. However, I only had a few minutes to get to my English class and it was on the second floor. Post haste I ran up the stairs forgetting the mess I left inside the restroom, and while I looked like something the cat wouldn't bury, I ignored my personal attire.

I don't know how our teacher got the mess cleaned from the floor but the next day it was gone. Did she figure out the prankster who dislodged the contraption? Who knows…but she smiled when I walked into the classroom. I thought it might have been a smile of disdain but the way she laughed when I inspected the typewriter eased my mind. I was lucky not to have the same typewriter but wondered who the unlucky recipient was that received its wrath.

So long ago it was that these events happened but close at hand in that the computer is a spin off from an ancient machine to make our lives easier. Thankfully, my new computer is installed but getting used to its keyboard will take time as will the wide screen monitor. The old screen compressed my works but this one appears as a wide TV ... something strange and brightly eerie. The old keypad was "run in" conforming to my incessant typing but this new one...bless its arrival ... embraced my fingertips as though we were long lost friends.

Oh the bane of it all trapped by a computer but without it, where would I be? In the dark ages ... rewinding inky ribbons, unhinging sticking keys, using white out for errors, replacing airborne return modules, making carbon copies and taking a hammer to it when it balked. One of the most important things I hold dear ... I wouldn't be doing. It's writing these articles that keeps me in touch with all of you.

HALLOWEEN SCAVENGER HUNTS

Scavenger hunts can be fun as long as players adhere to rules and regulations and they stay within limits and boundaries. Hunts can be on any holiday but the one I remember most was during Halloween. It was the witching flight time where the moon outlined ghastly apparitions and ghouls hid to snatch wary children from safety.

We all know Halloween was meant to celebrate saints but somewhere along the way it became fun for children. Children don't think of lifting saintly spirits in praise or wait for the spirits to conjure the departed while the kids hold their breath in fear. It's a mind game, of sorts, as the living has a morbid delight in finding the scariest costume or mask to lie in wait for unsuspecting souls.

Most kids would brave the night and gulp down dry air in a desperate attempt to show their prowess for a bag of candy. Sometimes a kid got nothing as they stood dumfounded when asked to do a trick. I got wise and left off the "trick" to the well known phrase when I couldn't do a trick and wound up with a rock smashing the candy in my bag. I was never allowed to eat caramel popcorn balls or apples unless I knew the person who gave it to me. It took all I could muster to keep from crunching into a bright red apple. Apparently, other parents had qualms about them, too. The next day, you could see them scattered from one end of the ditch to the other. The morning after Halloween, they disappeared! Poof ... into thin air.

As I aged and put away the desire for bags of candy, the fun really began. The youth group at church decided to have a Halloween scavenger hunt. Adult organizers put together a list of objects we had to find within the hours of seven and nine o'clock. If we returned after nine o'clock, everything we found would be disqualified. The adults were adamant; we could not venture into Fort Smith as the items were placed in various areas of Van Buren. No roughhousing or misconduct would be tolerated. Two chaperones were stationed at the respective hiding places.

To denote proper hidden things, they were painted various colors. No substitutions would be accepted as initials of the organizers were penciled on them. If a group found an object, they had to leave a note telling other searchers it was no longer hidden. Piling into groups of four in various cars, we put our heads together to decipher the riddles. The hidden objects might be a bone, witches broom, black plastic caldron, or anything associated with Halloween. It would be a challenge.

See if you can work through two of my own cryptic renditions of today and figure out where I hid the bone and hat.

The cane is straight from the log did break; its crook is narrow bent. The railings iron, cast thin and tall, might shake or quake, if spent. One road is short, it stops dead-end, many secrets gathered there. The quietness of the common folk but listen they may share. The shadows strike, they do abound but cease when daylight breaks. Some are tall and others short these concrete and marble stakes. Don't despair; you are nearly there just one more little step and if you falter, if you fail do not hold your breath. To find the bone, look up look down and even all around. The simple trick, don't blink your eye; it's there upon the ground. The cross gives clue; it's due north but please don't go to park. Instead, back up and then stop short two paces east there from the arch.

To whom the bell tolls loud and clear, we don't know a name. It strikes a chord; the hour is near the seconds tick and clang. Around and round it never stops until the next refrain. The bong does sound it echoes loud, not cloaked there is no shroud. The ewer pours and water flows, a little narrow stream. The lady proud she stands erect awake in yon history's dream. Do not venture near ye soured brew ... some say its rancid roil. The bars hold back to those are sacked its tether holds the spoil. The meter clicks by a concrete path, the knoll is grassy green. Beyond due south you will find the staff, from outside they are not seen. When midnight turns from gray to black and bats fly on the prowl, you will find the hat below his marbled respected cowl.

All the clues were there. Did you figure out the areas of the bone and hat? You didn't need to leave your house to enjoy a scavenger hunt. Most people familiar with Van Buren will hone in on the two locations. If not, don't lose any sleep over it as the teenagers in my group had the same problem. We found a few of the illusive items but in the process wound up bleary eyed from reading the directions with a flashlight.

Growing up and putting away the need to trick or treat for candy, I found the trick (cryptic puzzle) more fascinating than gathering the treat. For me, scavenger hunts didn't include rocks inside sacks. The conundrum of one puzzle remains and gives great pause and glitch ... what happened to all those caramel popcorn balls and apples scattered in the ditch?

THE LEGEND OF SLEEPY HOLLOW

Two weeks before Halloween in 1953, Daddy began reading *The Legend of Sleepy Hollow* to my sister and me. The book happened to be one of Daddy's favorites. Zip through the weeks. It was Halloween night and black as coal tar outside our house. Daddy was at work and I think Mother, on this night, was happy to stay indoors because our young ages made her go with us to collect candy. The elements didn't allow us to go trick or treating so Mother opened the book.

Mysteriously it popped open on a page I wished stayed shut. This was one spooky night! The streetlight at the corner of Henry Street burned out, or if truth was known, shot out by a sling shot pellet. Lights on street corners were few and far between. The one on our corner looked like an upside down metal bowl with an exposed twenty watt bulb. It was oftentimes on the fritz with flickering, macabre undertones as shadows darted to and fro. Perhaps it was our imagination playing devious tricks on these ominous hours of darkness, but a few reflections from neighboring window lamps told another story.

A dim light we could see out our front door was the stubby candle's glow inside a pumpkin Daddy carved. Its interior light exaggerated the sharp toothed, grotesque face as it sat on a bench near the front door. It was rainy, dank and cold as the wind picked up, swirling leaves in all directions giving rise to scenes in the book. The pumpkin's candle extinguished and our front stoop turned dark.

Mother continued to read about Ichabod Crane, the school teacher with gangly arms and legs, flat head, green eyes, huge ears and scared stiff nature. He was superstitious and believed everything was out to get him. Hazel and I were engrossed and anxious to hear what happened when he met the headless horseman. It was short lived when a giant thud hit the top of our house. Mother slammed the book shut and slung it across the room. My hair was static electric, as if someone rubbed an air filled balloon atop my head. My sister's brown eyes grew large as saucers. Mother, usually the calm, cool and collected one, came unhinged as she jerked us up and hovered over us like the mother hen she was.

Like I said, Daddy was at work and unable to soothe our fears. He was an avid reader, ungodly maniacal prankster and collector of strange objects. Our house overran with grisly, blood curdling bits and pieces of his harboring. Before Daddy did a remodel, we lived in a three room house ... yes, I said three room house and we survived close quarters. Hanging above the front door was a sharp, two foot saber in its ugly, brown sheath. The handle had a silver curlicue reminiscent of those in medieval times. It gave light to suitors having a duel. All we needed to complete this scenario was the gray armor perched in a corner. Thank goodness it wasn't there. Hanging on a wall was a picture of the most horrid, eye chasing man ever to come down the pike. Every direction I walked, this hideous ruffle throated man with plumed hat watched me like a hawk. My sister and I hated the picture and felt our napes bristle with the hot penetrable eyes of this strange man. Daddy took delight in knowing this picture scared the beejeebers out of us deliberately creating heart palpitating moments. Mother wanted to kill him.

On this bizarre Halloween night, nothing could get worse, could it? Daddy should have been home an hour earlier but wasn't. Hazel and I dozed off and Mother sat impatiently for Daddy. Without warning, Mother let out an ear piercing Indian war whoop that would wake the dead. Hazel and I woke up and watched Mother as she ran around in circles. Back and forth to the window she ran, yelling there was a headless horseman on a white horse clopping down the street. We didn't believe her but she forced us to look out the window. So help me Hanna, as I live and breathe and may God strike me dead for lying, a white horse carrying a cloaked man without a head, stopped in front of our house. Mother was screaming bloody murder and it set off a chain reaction with Hazel and me in tune.

We watched in trepidation as the headless horseman raised his hand and flung a damned old pumpkin toward the house. Splat and double splat as another pumpkin pelted the house. Mother did a double run when the pumpkin jolt made the nefarious sword fall to the floor. I never heard so many blue words coming out of my mother's mouth and didn't understand one word of them.

The horseman blared, "Bawahahaha." As fast as the horse appeared, it disappeared and so did the horseman. Then, outside the window we heard these words. "Did'ja hear thet, Ma?" Mother turned a ghastly shade of blue and almost took a tumble to the floor. We were scared speechless and I never wanted to look out the window again or hear about *The Legend of Sleepy Hollow*. Right then and there, there was enough legend on Henry Street.

About twenty minutes after the hoopla, Daddy sauntered through the front door. A huge grin plastered Daddy's face like the wide mouthed Cheshire cat in *Alice in Wonderland*. Mother began telling him about the headless horseman and he let off a belly laugh to rattle the rafters. Mother was livid because he continued laughing. We kept telling him it was the truth, there was a headless horseman and someone was outside our window. To appease us, he walked around the house, came back and said it was a bunch of nonsense. Hazel and I blurted. "What about the pumpkins?" Without blinking an eye, Daddy reached inside his jacket, pulled out a small pumpkin, flung his jacket above his head and yelled like a banshee. "Bawahahaha."

By then, it was too late. We knew it was him and his secret unraveled. We listened as he told us he knew Mother would read us the story. Borrowing a horse, he said he went up and down the street twenty times before Mother had the courage to peer out the window. My daddy, the proverbial prankster, pulled off one of the most insidious tricks of Halloween. He watched, in the shadows of darkness, as we, his prey, lived the horrors of *The Legend of Sleepy Hollow*.

SASSAFRAS TEA

Growing up in Frog Holler, Mother knew all kinds of trees and plants. She told me about planting potatoes on a rocky hillside and stacking rows of rocks somewhat like those of Ireland and New England. She told me if she never saw a rock again, it would be too soon. I laughed because I love rocks and have them all over my yard.

The one thing I remember most is her telling me about the Sassafras tree. It's a fragrant blossoming tree in the spring with yellowish green flowers, deep rich colors in the fall and edible blue/black berries. Critters of all kinds would forage the leaves, eat the berries in the summer and chew on the bark in the winter to stay alive. It was one way to know if something was poison. If critters, such as deer, rabbits, bear and other wild animals survived on the laurel, so could humans. Crushed leaves smell of citrus and when you pulverize dried leaves, you can use it to thicken soups and gumbo. Call it filé gumbo.

Mother could recognize the leaves and the bark as we traveled through the countryside. In the spring, the leaves, on a single branch, can be two lobed (looking somewhat like a child's mitten), oval, or with three fingered points. It's a distinct branching limb. In winter, the bark of a mature tree is a thick, dark reddish brown color and the younger trees host a brownish orange color. Because sassafras tree roots sprout in fencerows, it spreads like the plague making it a nuisance to farmers in cultivated soil.

The tree can grow tall, about 50 to 120 feet but the root runners spread all over the place making small brushy plants. It was these small trees Mother enjoyed most. It was not so much for their beauty but for the tree roots. Every winter, when the sap flowed downward to the roots, Mother, Daddy, and my sister and I would go sassafras hunting.

Bundled up like Eskimos to keep from freezing to death inside Daddy's old car, we wound up in the boonies near Devil's Den. Half the time the old car heater wouldn't work and when it did, Mother would crank down a window to keep from suffocating. Our coats were on and off like a flipped light switch. Out of nowhere Mother would yell, "Stop." Now, being on a dirt road and angled toward a ditch, Daddy would slam on the brakes making the hair on the neck stand upright. In my opinion, those ditches we shot toward, as an arrow enroot to a bulls eye, appeared to be as deep as the Grand Canyon. Daddy would laugh like a hyena because he knew his royal American stunt scared the living daylights out of us. His ornery ways always pushed the envelope.

Pulling the car precariously toward the steep embankment, Mother would chastise him with a few choice black and blue words for not giving her room to exit the car. She had to scoot toward the driver's seat, hold the door open with her foot and grunt and groan to make her way. Hazel and I had to do likewise until Daddy fetched the pick and shovel from the trunk. Like all small children, Hazel and I dogged them down the ditch full of oversized jagged rocks and then through brush. Daddy, with the pick and shovel angled over his shoulder, would say, "Cille, are you sure it's the right tree?" She would give him a look of disdain and tell him not to dig at the tree but the small trees around it. This every year antic became "old hat" but the very first time I remember hunting sassafras roots, I thought they had buried gold or something under the tree. When they pulled up the roots, I thought they were lunatics but then, they were Mother and Daddy and earned the right to be stupid. My kids tell me I learned well.

Watching Daddy dig the roots and put them in an old gunnysack, the extracted roots radiated a delightful aroma. Some of the roots were young but Daddy always managed to unearth several old roots from the parent tree. I always wanted him to put the gunnysack in the floorboard near the back seat so I could enjoy wafting the scent toward my face. I couldn't wait to get home because I could help Mother wash the roots to free them from dirt so we could have sassafras tea.

Usually, Mother let the roots dry for about a week but my incessant "please" made her fix tea in a small quantity. The roots, steeped in boiling water, made a light pink liquid. Letting any sediment fall to the bottom of the pot, the water gently cooled. Straining the liquid through cheesecloth or muslin and placing the roots where they would dry for future use, Mother poured me a cup of tea. Adding a tad of sugar and milk, the tea was ready to enjoy.

Some things you think are good for you may not be. Sassafras tea came to an abrupt halt when Mother heard it might be carcinogenic. All the years we and other people drank tea from sassafras roots it's hard to believe it could do major harm but I am not a chemist in knowing the tree's properties. Grocery stores sometimes offer sassafras tree roots for sale but I pass them by as they don't have dirt on them, smell the same or come in gunnysacks. It's the memory of Mother and Daddy, cold weather, overcoats and deep ditches keeping me from their purchase. Besides, if I close my eyes ... I am there in my youth and all the memories of my fourth cup pink sassafras tea floods my taste buds as if it were yesterday.

BLACK AND WHITE TELEVISION

Back in the 1950's, some of the sitcoms would give today's shows a run for their money. Black and white films are my favorites because they leave the imagination open. Anyone wearing dark attire made you think. Were they wearing black or navy blue? Light colored clothing might be white or pastels. Were floral arrangements, sitting atop grand furniture in a foyer ... real or facsimile? Were the ornate objects, thrown at a misbehaving spouse, gold or silver? When a dire situation crept up in the script, musical transitions in modulating chords made the viewer realize someone was about to be attacked. Shadows in backgrounds meant to tell you there was someone or something pulling you into the mire of the scene. Only the mind could discern or delicately color objects on the set.

Several weekends ago, Dan and I watched a series of four Ma and Pa Kettle movies. Actually, we taped some of them to watch when re-runs of re-runs bored us senseless. As we sat there glued to the idiot tube watching Ma sweep the chickens out of the run down shack and Pa saying he would get around to repairing things in due time, I thought of many old shows.

Do you remember Leo G. Carroll, the British actor having roles in *The Man from U.N.C.L.E.* and Hitchcock films? He was Marley's ghost in *The*

Christmas Carol. The funniest role was Cosmo Topper with Lee Patrick playing the role of his wife in a hilarious sitcom. You might remember her as Sam Spade's sexy secretary in the 1941 film, *The Maltese Falcon.* The Topper's, he a bank executive and she a wacky spouse, purchased a grand mansion. Living inside the mansion was a ghostly couple who decided they were not dead from a skiing accident and wouldn't leave their magnificent surroundings. Cosmo Topper, the only person who saw the haunting duo, came unhinged seeing them float around and watching them perch on tables or staircase rungs. In several episodes, Mrs. Topper thought Cosmo was losing his mind as his conversational outbursts, directed to the duo, sent her running for the nearest aspirin bottle. Although the ghosts had fun making Cosmo's life a living hell, they did make certain their "friends" were safe from harm and victimizing schemes. They were good ghosts with a tinge of impishness. Each episode came alive as we watched the scenes on our old Zenith television.

Most all of us have heard the term, "Living the life of Riley." Generally, we think of it as goldbricking, lazy people or a "kept" person living off someone else's hard-earned money. Then again, it might be someone having an extravagant life style with an advantage we covet. When I first saw the television show, *Life of Riley*, all I envisioned was Chester A. Riley being a klutzy, kindhearted man getting into all kinds of trouble. William Bendix, the man with a smile larger than an unpeeled banana and eyes soft as a wad of cotton personified Chester A. Riley. Raspy voiced, Bendix delivered his role as a bumbling, geesh, and I don't mean any harm but get me in trouble anyway, neighborhood nut. His cohort to major disasters and the instigator of hot water jams was friend / enemy Gillis, (Tom D'Andrea) a next-door neighbor. The wives for this undeniably, hysterical sitcom included Marjorie Reynolds as Peg Riley and Gloria Blondell as Honeybee Gillis.

Announcing itself as "America's funniest comedy show" was *I Married Joan*. It was the most rib aching, gut churning, eye watering, non-stop laughing show I ever watched ... except for *I Love Lucy*. Joan Davis, a brilliant comedy actress, played the part of Joan Stephens. Keeping her given name on the show, her real life daughter, Beverly Wills, also had a role in the show as Joan's sister. Jim Backus ... we all know him as the myopic Mr. Magoo and Thurston Howell III in *Gilligan's Island*...had the leading male role as Bradley Stevens, a laid-back, slow talking...pull the words out of my mouth, judge.

Joan, the idiotic, almost insane wife of Judge Bradley, couldn't keep her nose out of community business and tried to ruin the judge's stately decorum. Joan, in her attempt to show her prowess in being a know-it-all, was an accident looking for a place to crash. In my opinion, if Joan tried to climb an east side mountain to find a soothing drink, she would have slid down the west side head first into a vat of boiling water. She appeared to be as thick as a brick and unable to fight her way out of a paper bag, giving rise to brilliant audience appeal. Her knowledge as an actress and uncanny approach in knowing when to be the "straight man" in a scene, threw audiences into rigors.

Jim Backus had to have some type of title so they dubbed him Judge Bradley. Apparently, the script didn't call him to sit on a bench or hand down sentences to any wayward child or criminal. I often wondered why he could not have been a normal husband to throw up his hands in disgust with Joan's insanity. I suppose, in the end, his story telling and summations for Joan's escapades made the television sitcom.

These and many shows of the 50's were in black and white. They were not grandiose in exotic behavior nor did they suck face like a vacuum cleaner. The ending was not a cliffhanger but ended with a soothing solution. A simple, funny and clean movie for entire family viewing is what they were. Now, I think I will pop Ma and Pa back in the DVD, laugh until my guts hurt, let my imagination run rampant and color them the way I see it. Hmm ... is that rooster's tail iridescent blue/green or black?

QUIET

Quiet signs dotted every table and ends of shelves. Out of respect for people sitting at the tables perusing their favorite material, everyone entering the premises tried to obey rules. Oftentimes, the shiny waxed floor creaked under the weight of invading searchers creating a disdainful leer from those rattled from deep thoughts. You could feel scathing eyes penetrate your every move. Most of us knew the paths we could walk without unleashing a barrage of squeaks and moans. It was not our fault or wishes to interfere in another person's space. Blame it on the aging floorboards.

It was built in 1903 and known as The Old School Presbyterian Church but for its age, it was a lovely small old building. For me and many citizens of Van Buren, 421 Webster Street was our library. The Gothic windows and front entrance reminded me of a time of the Greek mythological Minotaur and centaurs and medieval gargoyles. Outside the front door lay an ugly, dark brown floor mat with bristles having the appearance of a heavy duty push broom. I knew when many patrons visited the aging building as dusty footprints, large and small, piled atop each other on the old hardwood floor. Either no one used the antiquated doormat or it was past salvaging as it didn't catch intended dust and dirt particles.

This old building was a refuge for many. Musty as it was with old books from days gone by and those by current authors mingled together. It created worlds of venues by traveling through gold leafed pages to other parts of the globe. Your mind could wander in exciting places to go, and at the same time, watch natives near a jungle hut, as they wrapped raw foods inside taro leaves to cook. The building held intrigue with its mystifying structure and so did its contents. Each day was different and exciting.

During the sixth grade, the class was introduced to classic literature. I wasn't sure if the classics would be something to enjoy but this particular book enthralled me. It was, unfortunately, not a book on the school shelf but designed in a classroom workbook by the teacher. We were allowed portions every other week while the teacher managed to update our individual workbooks. This piecemeal reading material was too slow for me as it whetted my appetite to reveal the plot.

In order to read more, I devoted time at the library. My stay was an hour long but the after school event allowed me to expand my mind. Going through the south door, my feet stayed to the right side of the small quarters until I reached the farthermost northeast corner of the building. A couple of my friends, having the same idea, selected books from *The Bobbsey Twins* series. They were stories of two sets of fraternal twins, Bert and Nan, age 12 and six year old siblings, Flossie and Freddie. While I enjoyed *The Bobbsey Twins* with the author letting us grow up with them in age, and

Nancy Drew and the Hardy Boys, I left them on the shelf in search of my secret.

Each day I went to the library, I held my breath hoping no one checked out the book. My friend was still there waiting for me to let him escape. No one bothered him as my next page lay undisturbed. The single strand of long blond hair, hinged between allergies laden, unread delectable words, let my fingers find the next chapter. Escape he did, telling me why his life turned to shambles and for me to take pity on his misfortunes. The book, published in 1861 by George Eliot (pen name of Mary Ann Evans) was *Silas Marner: The Weaver of Raveloe*. Set in the United Kingdom, the book knits its way through tragedy, pain and suffering. The main character, Silas anguished in being accused of stealing and losing the love of his life, leaves his hometown of Lantern Yard. Winding up a recluse, he settles in Raveloe where he loses his hoard of money through thievery and dastardly deeds of others. The book threads humor, love and hope through a mire of conflict and ultimately ends with resolving rewards. Every page of this book was picture perfect with thatched roofs, tattered clothes, gruel inside black pots, knitted gloves with missing fingers and foggy weather to make the mystery unfold. The fictional town of Lantern Yard conjured up eerie pictures. Marner, a weaver by trade, settled in Raveloe ... weaver and ravel ... were those words chosen by the author an accident or deliberate?

If not for my teacher, the classics would have no specific meaning. If George Eliot had not penned *Silas Marner: The Weaver of Raveloe*, I wouldn't have trekked through his world of the United Kingdom. Envisioning a timeframe, faraway places and habitat would be dormant. If construction workers didn't build The Old School Presbyterian Church with its marvelous structure, the library I came to enjoy wouldn't have been. Without the library to fuel my imagination, Gothic places and *Silas Marner* wouldn't be unleashed. There would be no voice or visions to fuel an inquisitive imaginative little girl so many years ago. Today, libraries are large and full of activity. The children are anxious with a burning desire to learn. Isn't it nice everything happens and falls in place for a reason?

In my mind, I still see those quiet signs in the quaint library and shadows of dusty footprints.

LONG BELL METHODIST EPISCOPAL CHURCH, SOUTH MOVERS and SHAKERS 1893

Reference in part: Historical Summary - Council on Ministries - Yearbook 1977

Van Buren was full of movers and shakers before the year 1893. W.S. Newman was the original leader of a community Sunday school. He held service on a portion of the grounds of what is now J.J. Izard Elementary School. Situated under large trees, a congregation gathered making it necessary to construct a permanent church building. It was not until the fall of 1893 that several members had an insight for the beginning of what many people would call Long Bell Methodist Episcopal Church, South.

Mrs. Matilda Newman, the mother of W.S., hosted those persons who would later join, as a whole, to see the building have its first corner stone erected.

They were Rev. and Mrs. S.M. Kelton, Mrs. J.B. Paine, Dr. and Mrs. W.L. Gullette and Mrs. S.A. Miller. Later, at a second meeting to confirm construction, additional persons attended. They were Mr. S.A. Miller, Mr. J.B. Paine, and Mr. and Mrs. M.F. Smeltzer. A charter membership, made of these eleven persons, finalized the church's position.

The chosen site was at 20th and Emma Streets. With the expertise of W.S. Newman, a master carpenter, the church was completed. The reason the church had the name Long Bell Methodist Episcopal Church, South was because it was near a mill operated by Long Bell Lumber Company. Areas of Van Buren took on monikers of people or business that occupied particular regions. The first minister to stand at the pulpit was the Rev. S.M. Kelton. An accomplished bricklayer by profession, Kelton pastured the church by the appointment of Presiding Elder Rev. S.S. Key. As the church grew in attendance, the need for a parsonage to house residing ministers and family was a necessity. The parsonage, completed in 1896, was located west of the church. Second minister, Rev. Coward, and his wife was the first family to occupy the parsonage. It was a small parsonage and filled the need until the year 1960 when Rev. Bill Wilder got the ball rolling and helped in planning the new parsonage. A decision, made by members of the church, was to move the original house to an area directly behind the old church and rent it for public use.

Later in 1921, the original church moved to North 20th Street for use as a residence. Had it not been for Mr. and Mrs. Jess N. Evans, Sr., having the foresight to move the old church, the new facility might have laid dormant. The congregation, in accord, felt the need to build a larger church south of the original church to accommodate more people. New construction began in 1921 after a loan, for $600.00, secured the purchase of two lots from C.A and H.F. Pape and Mrs. F.R. McKibben. A third lot came in the form of a donation. These three lots, excavated to provide a basement for the church, are located at 20th Street and Alma Boulevard.

Drafter and director of the plans was Mr. J.B. Paine. A committed desire and volunteer labor helped complete the basement. Because men had day jobs, the construction was during night hours. The women of the church did their job as well. Their kitchens cranked out cookies, sandwiches and drinks for the workers. For one year, basement services filled congregational needs until the brick structure was complete in 1924. Mr. Leslie Campbell, a bricklayer, laid each brick surrounding the exterior. Interior design and construction, done by Mr. W.S. Newman, had an ornate tin ceiling with cherubs on the surround of light fixtures. The church debt, erased in 1928 under the Reverends Earl Cravens and H. Lynn, allowed the 172 members to enjoy a church dedication.

Circuit riders serviced Long Bell Methodist Episcopal Church, South. It was common for a single pastor, on horseback, to travel a twenty-five mile radius to hold various services. The church went through name changes. What people called Long Bell changed to East Van Buren Methodist Episcopal Church, South. Then, in 1950, the name became St. John's United Methodist Church while Rev. Floyd G. Villines, Jr. filled the pulpit. A year later, the church began with full time ministers.

St. John's was a wonderful old church. Changes made to the interior structure were updating surrounds on the stain glass windows (all memorials with plaques) and painting walls a lighter shade. You could feel the love and compassion in memorials. A rose window installed above the choir loft, a nursery stain glass for little Pam Wilder, daughter of Rev. and Mrs. Wilder, a piano in loving memory to my mother-in-law, Naomi Rapier and wall chimes for Joey Burkhart helped ease pain. The basement, sectioned off for Sunday school classes, secured the need for a fellowship hall. Attached to the educational building's south exit, the hall saw many delightful men's breakfasts, spaghetti suppers, pie sales and meetings.

The concept of a church so many years ago laid the foundation for success. Families who were raised and worshiped in this small building enjoyed life to its fullest. Sometimes laughter pealed through the roof but tears ... those gut wrenching tears flowed as a river as souls soared from our grasp. As life dissipates in the coming of years, so did this marvelous church. The building, mere mortar and brick, continues to stand but the members, "the church," no longer walk its hallowed halls.

Stay tuned ... more to come.

BATS, IRISH JIGS & TURNIP GREENS

For many years, St. John's United Methodist Church proudly sat on the corner of 20th & Alma Boulevard. Dan and I met there in the late 50's and then our family continued through the 80's until it merged with First United Methodist Church to form Heritage United Methodist Church. It was a small church where everyone laughed, prayed and sang together.

On occasion, during church service, a bat swooping from the ornate ceiling would disrupt the calm atmosphere. Bats loved the open vents at the top of the church and used the nook and crannies within the attic to roost. It didn't matter what type of material we used to plug entrances. The bats, having the ability to squeeze through pin sized holes, continued to fly devilish acts while a hell's fire and damned nation's sermon filled the sanctuary. We knew, when the preacher cranked out fiery sermons and smacked the podium, a visit was in the making.

The only time women were rattled was when a Wednesday evening potluck or spaghetti supper had an intrusive visit by an unwanted bat. The men, seeing our plight, would catch the bats and release them unharmed. All of these events, held in the basement of the church before the fellowship hall was constructed, made hilarious Key Stone Cop routines. Unfortunately, when the women planned spaghetti suppers for the public, a visitor might exude a high-pitched screech while her hair stood on end. One man, feeling something crawl up the outside of his pants leg, did an Irish Jig between tables when he realized a bat was inching closer to his crotch. Situated at the west end of the basement, the kitchen would be hotter than a firecracker on July when the stove belched heat. Even with air-conditioning, the temperature was atrocious. However, we didn't mind as Wednesday evening potluck suppers brought tempting home cooked foods.

David Scroggin, appointed in 1972, was our minister. He was gregarious, evangelical and appealed to the younger generation. Under his leadership, there was a need to expand as members grew. In order to accommodate the numbers, an expansion to the church was set forth. November 1975, a plan for a new fellowship hall came to fruition. It was exciting but before construction could begin in 1976, the church had to raise 33% of the indebtedness.

In one month, the building fund raised $17,596.50 and exceeded the percentage. Each consecutive month, the members increased targets. By 1977, members came through and paid off the total cost of construction as well as a new parking lot. Those two endeavors pushed forth re-modeling of the education building built in 1950. It didn't stop there. Sectioned off to make six large rooms, the basement housed four Sunday school classes, a library and the other a film room. Every square inch of the church had a purpose for ministry and outreach.

The women of the church loved the new fellowship hall. It was equipped with up to date appliances and room to work. Spaghetti suppers, held on Friday before the first ball game of the season, kept us busy. Paula Williams and I wiped out Olin Smith Grocery Store of a certain type of spaghetti and hit John Garner Meats on Rudy Road for great ground beef. Part of our sauce was complete. Mr. & Mrs. Hays, of Hay's Grocery Store at 15th and Main Street, always donated tomato sauce, spices and French bread. They did it with a smile and conveyed well wishes. With our cars loaded to the brim, we sped back to the fellowship hall to concoct our special homemade spaghetti sauce. Our recipe made enough servings for six hundred people and before the night ended, we scraped the bottom of the pots and hoped a last minute hungry eater didn't open the door. It was seldom having leftovers but if we did, we took it to the Gospel Rescue Mission. We discarded nothing.

The baked pie sales went great. Lavelle Garr, the ramrod of the event, was a real enterprising person. We called her "Garvelle" due to Darrell Williams messing up her name. One year I made one hundred thirteen pie shells, froze and toted them to the church. Others did likewise. Garvelle and other women, on an assembly line, filled them to the brim with delectable fillings. Orders came and went out the door as fast as the oven could bake them. On occasion, Garvell would laugh and say her husband, Gene, dropped a pie in the floor and we would have to eat it. Lavelle and Gene were one of a kind and their hearts were big as all outdoors. I miss both of them.

Beans, greens and cornbread suppers were fun. Have you ever put greens in your bathtubs? If not ... do not! Paula and I filled our bathtubs full of turnip greens to wash grit from the leaves. It was a mess when the water needed to be changed. Have you ever slung wet greens into a large trash bag? Don't entertain the thought or you will regret it because we had more greens on our floor and clothing than what went into the bag. Not only that, but your house reeks with the residue of the aftermath. With all the greens piled into each our tubs, it wilted down into one large pot. We had a ball doing things for the benefit of our church but it was time for change.

St. John's United Methodist Church with all its good and bad times was remarkable. This gold leaf page of history closed as it did many years ago. You have to move forward as time waits for no man.

JOLT FROM JALEPENO PEPPERS

If my car had a "smell-a radiator" in the form of a homing device, it would automatically go to Sharon and Larry Black's farm when tomatoes get ripe. It's a good thing I am in control of the four wheels or I might not make it back home. Go ahead, pitch me a tent in the tomato fields and I will be a happy camper.

Today was my second visit to purchase another 40 pounds of the delectable, homegrown beauties. As usual, my kitchen had an aroma of fiery salsa cooking, and mace, from jalapeños and salsa peppers, sent me reeling toward the overhead stove vent. I love the taste of hot peppers. It's the kind of pepper making the hairs in the nose do a cha-cha on the floor while saluting nasal and sinus cavities. I don't care much for habaneros because they have a scorched flavor and the 200,000 - 300,000 Scoville units of heat per pepper will melt paint off a car. Yep, they are hotter than a pistol-packing mama and they can jolly well stay on the vine.

Pleasant Valley Road, where Sharon and Larry live, is a busy road this time of year. I do believe everyone in the county knows about the farm and if not ... anyone reading this will. As I pulled out of their driveway going toward Highway 64, I remembered Newt, Claude and Floyd Black. Each of the Black's was in close proximity to each other. The vast fields behind each house were a haven for many types of vegetables.

I began laughing as I remembered how my sister-in-law, Paula Williams, and I would pack our children in our cars and zip down the narrow lane to the cabbage crop behind Claude's house. With a sharp hatchet, we would smack the heads of cabbage and sling them into baskets in our trunks. Secure, knowing we had enough to make gallons of sauerkraut; we left the field and went to Paula's yard.

Outside, near her garage, we began slicing cabbage like mad women on a rampage. Before the day was over, each of us had at least fifty gallons each. Why, in our right minds, did we think any family needed fifty gallons of sauerkraut? Before we devoured all the sauerkraut, I swore never to put up another gallon jar of the spit popping, teeth grinding sour stuff. Besides, my kids' eyes began to water at the thought of another mouthful and moaned when they saw a jar on the cabinet. Why did we have so many gallon jars? It was because we put up tons of pickles and pickled okra and our houses reeked of vinegar. Take my word for it; our children never had the need for any type of artificial laxative.

A few yards down the road, my hysterical laughter ceased. Wiping my teary eyes and composing myself, the wheels on my car whipped to the right. It was a response to reading the vegetable sign. My brain and wheels are in accord when roadside vendors come into view. It isn't the first time my car took it upon itself to visit this place as last year, it did the same.

On the narrow counter were onions, zucchini, eggplant, purple hull peas, new potatoes, tomatoes, jalapeños and salsa peppers. I honed in on the peppers, as I needed them for my salsa. I asked if they were hot and she said yes. Popping a jalapeño in my mouth, it had a small bite but not hot enough for my pleasure. Picking up a bright red salsa pepper, I bit off a chunk. It was a tad hotter so I decided to buy both varieties. I couldn't resist the onions so they became part of my purchase. Behind the counter and hanging on the wall of the shed were pieces of farm equipment. They were part of this family's past and used while farming their forty acres.

Mrs. Jenkins wore a pink blouse and blue Capri's and sported a visor atop her beautiful white hair. She told me her husband, Bill, and she farmed the acreage for many years. Looking across the fields, I spied cabbage! I squelched the desire to come unhinged with laughter because she wouldn't understand my insanity. When I told her where I bought my tomatoes, she asked if the Black's were relatives. On my husband's side was my response. She then went on to tell me how she and Bill, along with Claude, Floyd, and Newt, would take squash to Stillwell for processing. It was many years ago but still vivid in her mind. Stilwell frozen vegetables were staples in many deep freezes, mine included. No doubt, my family ate part of their squash crop as Stilwell Products, in Stilwell, Oklahoma, had great frozen vegetables. Stilwell Products sold their enterprise to Flowers Industries, Inc. in 1976.

She and I talked about how the weather affected all crops. She said she could take the rain in moderation but watching the heat steam the vines was devastating. She then went on to say. "All farmers have to contend with the same natural calamities. It's a part of farming you can't get past and you have to live with what nature decides to do." It's a fact and I have great regard for a farmer's tenacity and respect their hard work. I enjoyed speaking with her and locked away this special memory of her standing behind the counter in the small shed. I won't forget her smile and will think of her each time a salsa jar is opened. It will be her jalapeño and salsa peppers giving my children and friends a jolt.

WORLDBURGER & GRANDBURGER & TAMALES

At the curve, as you entered Tenth Street from Midland going south into Fort Smith, a large building had a high fence with signs. Bright arrows, attached to the fence along with metal barriers near its perimeter, indicated caution. Many drivers, going too fast around this dangerous curve, plowed through the business. I remember Daddy approaching the curve and hoped the treacherous area would magically straighten. My sister and I were in the back seat of his old coupe wondering where he would stop. It was a busy street with various businesses dotting the narrow lane and at each intersection was, what we called, ocean waves. The ocean waves, higher than ordinary speed bumps, made the stomach churn if a driver exceeded the speed limit. I think people in the know erected them to keep kids from wanting to eat, because many good restaurants and drive-in's were in the area. The aroma was enough to tempt any taste bud.

Did you ever eat a Worldburger? If not, you missed one of the tastiest burgers of all times. Almost three times the size of a regular hamburger, the condiments on top the special beef made it lip smacking good. Worldburger was on the corner of

10th & H Streets and it allowed for many vehicles and occupants to enjoy watching carhops balance meals while on roller skates. As a child, I didn't have a clue who owned the establishments. The burgers were so large; Daddy cut one in half for my sister and me. It was a special treat and I relished every morsel. It was not until the 1970's that Dan and I met Dub Bromley at St. John's United Methodist Church. He owned the Worldburger's on Tenth Street and Towson Avenue. We became very good friends and every time he came to visit us, he brought bags of Worldburgers to our house. He would smile and say, "Pop these in the freezer. When you get hungry you can warm them in the oven." He knew I was in Worldburger heaven. R.I.P., Dub Bromley.

On down Tenth Street is Grand Avenue. Daddy would veer toward the east and I knew he was going to The Grand at 12th and Grand Avenue for bakery doughnuts or to Harry Marsh on the corner of 14th and Grand Avenue. Harry Marsh's Grandburger was not a hamburger but delectable pulled beef with a sauce. It had lettuce but no condiments, as it didn't need any. The sauce tasted somewhat like thin catsup, but according to the recipe Mr. Marsh gave me, it's not mere catsup.

One day while in Hays Grocery Store, Mr. Marsh and I began talking. I told him I enjoyed eating his burgers and slugging down his homemade vanilla shakes. He remembered my mother and dad, and two gangly girls anxiously waiting for his prepared feast. It was a feast, as we didn't often eat anywhere other than at home. Standing there in the grocery store, I watched as Mr. Marsh took an envelope from his jacket pocket. He took out its contents, began scribbling on its exterior and then handed me the envelope. Imagine my surprise when I realized it was his recipe for Grandburger. It was an added treat or "feast" to add his recipe to my collection of great foods. I will always treasure this gift and remember his remarkable, one of a kind burger.

Going down Eleventh Street toward Van Buren, another stop to whet the appetite was Shorty McCurdy Tamales. Shorty's store was on the corner of G Street. It was an unassuming store with comic books lining the front window. A person could trade or buy the latest comics while waiting on the homemade tamales. Perfectly made with masa de maize, a cornmeal used in authentic Spanish tortillas, tamales and other dishes, the tamales nested in warm corn shucks. Shorty sold them by the dozen and when I asked him how long it took to make tamales, I was amazed to find out "several hours." He told me he had to cook, seed, and scrape the guajillo peppers for the sauce. While the massive amount of pulverized meat cooked, he prepared the masa using a portion of the pepper liquid and other spices to make smooth dough. He rolled paper-thin dough inside soaked corn shucks, filled them with meat filling and then steamed them until done. His unique technique in making tamales had people swarming in and out of the store.

I never tried to master the Worldburger. Dub's winning burger was special. Even though he told me the secret of his burger, my house didn't have the atmosphere of his drive-in or the grill. Even with the recipe from Mr. Marsh, the Grandburger didn't taste as it did when I was a child. My tamales were good even though it took forever and a day to concoct but they were not Shorty's. There are knock off recipes galore on the internet with people determined to attain a taste they remember as a child. Some things you can't duplicate, no matter how hard you try. Maybe it's for the best because personalities and hands making these special dishes ... you can't copy. Here's to you: Dub Bromley, Mr. Harry Marsh and Shorty McCurdy for making my memories special.

THE BIG GIANT

The Big Giant was a large warehouse. The front of the store (on Main Street) had large windows, sometimes dirty, sometimes clean. Placards, advertising various specials, dotted the windows. The signs were bright yellow or red and the word "save" was printed in bulky letters.

It was the place to go if you wanted a bargain. Located where the Crawford County Jail stands, you entered through heavy double doors to find a multitude of items. Canned goods to dry goods filled every nook and cranny. Women, searching for notions, swarmed through sewing material and patterns to make the latest fashion. Around Christmas, the perimeter was stacked with all kinds of toys, tinsel and believe it or not aluminum Christmas trees. The tips of silver trees peeked from the tops of boxes and some, sitting on the floor for purchase, were fashioned with decorations.

Little kids danced around in anticipation of what they might find under their tree ... especially if they found a bright red wagon tucked away between isles. An occasional "sold" tag could be seen tied to handles and an "oh no" could be heard slipping from the mouths of children. They were crushed to learn their coveted Christmas present wouldn't be waiting for them on Christmas day.

Memorial wreaths were stacked on top of each other covering an area from the floor to ceiling. If you wanted a particular wreath, chances are, it was one of a kind and on the bottom of the stack. Not to worry though, the sales ladies would make certain you received it before you left the premises. The Big Giant was the place to be when you wanted an item or enjoy the atmosphere of unusual items.

The other day I was in need of some flower pots. Don't know why because my yard is full of flowers. It was an urge to add more plants to a square inch not filled in Joyce's Jungle. I thought of the Big Giant and how, if I needed an off the wall item, I could find it there. The only alternative was to drive to Alma's, A-Z.

If you have never been to A-Z, make sure you pack a lunch to last for four days because you need to take your time perusing. It's impossible to look at everything in one day and I wished I had one week to cram into an hour shopping. A-Z has a restaurant, furniture store and a giant warehouse full of unusual items. The buildings are brilliant white and a donkey wearing blinders couldn't miss them. The white buildings pull you into the parking lot, somewhat like a magnet. It seems to be a rather innocent entrance until you step inside and then, as your eyes adjust, it's overwhelming. Was I in Loompaland? Although I am not a male, I felt like an Oompa-Loopa, a fictional character in Roald Dahl's, *Willy Wonka and the Chocolate Factory* ... where would I go first? It was a tasty adventure without the chocolate.

In the east quad are tons of artificial flowers, knick knacks and whatnots. If you can't find what you are looking for, take my word for it, you don't need it. They have employees who design beautiful floral arrangements and wreaths. Tooling on down the aisles I ran across garden accessories, bedding, groceries, sundries, carpet and furniture, toiletries and make-up, country-western items and Safari objects. Anything you can imagine ... imagine it in A-Z. It's a hodgepodge, a virtual great idea packed into a warehouse ... like the Big Giant ... only larger and exciting.

A massive array of flower pots, all shapes, sizes and different components could be found along each isle but not what I envisioned. Knowing what I wanted my search wouldn't end. As I neared the carpet and furniture area, a stack of half barrel pots caught my attention. They were perfect. Resembling an old fashioned pickle keg with metal rims around the center, they would be the pieced de résistance for my begonias. It took me a while to find them but it was a delightful search. Checking out, I told a Mountainburg resident, who was a checker for A-Z to wait a minute. She didn't know me from Adam. Handing her my driver's license for check verification, she glanced at me. She recognized my name. "I may not know you but I read your articles in the *Press Argus - Courier*. I like to read *Times Record*, Sharon Randall, too."

Now, you could have knocked me over with a feather because I don't walk up to people and tell them I am a guest columnist for the Press Argus - Courier. To be mentioned in the same breath with Sharon Randall and have someone remotely think I write like her is a major compliment. Hearing the checker tell me she read my articles made my day.

If I hadn't needed flower pots, I may not have gone to A-Z and I probably wouldn't have met her. Sometimes I think paths are meant to be crossed because it's when we don't expect the expected we meet fabulous people. This day was great. I found my containers, met a lovely lady and I stepped back in time thinking of the Big Giant by a new name ... A-Z.

CITY PARK & ACTIVITIES
Ah, the smell of chlorine

It was sweltering as it is today. Kids didn't care about the hot temperature or if old sol blistered their skin. They didn't want to hear the weather forecast on the radio or scan the newspaper to read a listing. Time was wasting and lines would be forming. Not to mention, for those who had cars the good parking spots would be gone. If you were lucky and knew someone who drove, you might catch a ride. If not, the "dogs" took over and you hoofed it to the park.

Turning into the City Park, you could almost smell the chlorine in the swimming pool as it beckoned kids to hurry up and take a dive. Paying minimal coins to the cashier, girls went to the right and boys went to the left. Greeted by a changing room and a few lockers for excess clothing, modesty didn't seem to be an issue as street clothes flew in all directions. We were anxious to get into the swimming suit. Spraying water hit you before you entered the pool area making you gasp.

The swimming pool was L shaped with a high fence surrounding its perimeter. A kiddy's pool, separated from dangerous depths, offered shallow water for moms and tots. The pool, packed to the brim on a hot summer's day, was dotted with bright psychedelic bath towels. A bottle containing a mixture of baby oil and iodine was the "Coppertone" of our era. The iodine turned our skin a shade of streaked orange and the baby oil made us slippery. After a while in the blistering sun, you couldn't tell where the orange stopped and the sunburn began. One good thing, we all looked alike in the lobster boil.

The lifeguards were our safety net. Whistles, hung around their necks, gave off penetrating tweets when an overzealous kid decided to run on the wet concrete. The swimming pool was more than a pool to idle time away or work on a tan. The lifeguards, there to maintain control, sat on laddered platforms. They were popular with the crowd as everyone knew them from school but they were doing a job ... a serious job keeping everyone safe.

The lifeguards offered swimming lessons for children eager to learn how to do the basic dogpaddle. The kids learned more techniques each time they went for a lesson and were proud of achievements. The time spent in teaching swimming lessons was more than a typical learning experience for kids. It brought families together in a structured atmosphere where everyone was educated. It was common to see parents or relatives sitting in a covered pavilion cheering their child toward victory. Yes, our swimming pool was small and antiquated but it was a great place to be during the summer. It captured a time to remember our youth. I was glad my three children were able to enjoy the pool but gradually it succumbed to vandals and deteriorated beyond repair. Sad isn't it we don't have a pool for kids to build memories but then, would a new pool be cost effective?

The pool wasn't the only activity in the park. Do you remember the miniature golf course we called putt-putt? A small concession stand was near the entrance where you paid your entry fee. The course was under massive oak trees offering shade and an occasional squirrel would chatter at intrusive people. On Saturday and Sunday, the area was swarming with kids and adults plying their skill in hitting a small golf ball to its intended target. There were windmills to avoid, puddles of water, wagon wheels and a maze of castled orifices. Often, too eager to master the ball, it would veer down into the wooded area making a search nearly impossible. The itchy vine called "dermatitis avoidant" or "scratch till you can't scratch anymore" would unmercifully grapple you by the leg or arm and waylay you with its power to rule.

There were sandboxes for kids, swings, teeter-totters, a jungle gym, and a place for horseshoe games. Picnic tables were always in use with families on an afternoon outing. Small hiking trails led to a stream where kids searched for crawdads, and if you were adventurous, you might hike to Eagle's Nest, the highest point in the city park northeast of the pool. The old cannon, near the pool, captivated small children as they played on it until the sun made it unbearable to touch. The boys and girls club provided tons of activities for kids. Several times, the park held Fourth of July fireworks by lighting up the sky in celebrating our nation's birth.

Times have changed. The park, at one time, was Van Buren City Park but now it is Dr. Louis Peer Memorial Park with a beautiful tribute at the entrance on Eleventh Street. There are still play areas for children with swings, slides and such. Multiple picnic areas dot scenic views. There is no poison ivy but meticulous groomed green areas. Now renovated, the boys and girls club looks great providing needed venues for children eager to learn and exercise.

Canadian geese swim magnificently in the lake adding interest for everyone. Jogging trails around the lake allow for exercise and the view is spectacular. Although there is no public swimming pool, these other great enjoyable areas will build lasting memories. Van Buren citizens have a city park to be proud of and it's what you have that is important ... not what you think you need ... that will make a person happy.

CRAWFORD COUNTY GENEALOGICAL SOCIETY, INC.

Genealogical Society on Key

Taking advantage of nice weather several days ago, I was hauling compost to my flowerbeds and vegetable garden. Dan, my better half, told me I had received a phone call and to return her call as soon as possible. I did and spoke to Dyer resident Mary Lou Kelly. She asked if I would speak at the next meeting of the Crawford County Genealogical Society. I have no trouble speaking but wondered what I might say to all the learned professional data collectors. My expertise in this field is not vast but I agreed to speak.

Tuesday, June 12, as I pulled into the narrow alleyway behind the Alma Public Library, Mary Lou Kelly and Wanda Aldridge were exiting a vehicle. Mary's beautiful smile and Wanda's gentle nod was all it took to make me feel right at home. To enter the premises, a white picket fence greets all who walk through to gain knowledge. Walking a few more paces, it almost felt as if I had entered a solarium. Surrounding the back door and its perimeter, flowers and potted plants dressed the brick patio giving off a welcoming gesture. Gentle raindrops hit the overhang while the plants bowed their heads. It was lovely.

This rainy day didn't deter members to attend, as their duty to provide residents with information on

Crawford County, far surpassed a few rain drops. They were on a mission and they would succeed. Situated in the back of the Alma Public Library is a quaint room full of history. If walls could talk, I am sure it would fill volumes. One by one, I met fabulous people: President, Nadean Riley Bell, Vice President, Mary Lou Kelly, Treasurer, Melba Hill, Secretary /Historian, Katie Black, Director at Large, Billy Gale Morse (one of my high school teachers), Committee /Library, Lucille Titsworth (chaired the 2009 quilt show), Memorial Chair, Mary Sue Lowrimore, Editorial Publications, Don Wilcox, Marilyn Hawkins and Gail Cowart. There are so many members; I can't list them all.

"The Crawford County Genealogical Society, Inc. is an Arkansas nonprofit corporation. It is recognized under IRS code, section 501c.3, as a tax exempt organization. The purpose of the Society is to create and support interest in genealogy and history among citizens of Crawford County, AR and the surrounding area. Through monthly meetings, publications, and special activities, the Society provides for the exchange of ideas and technologies for genealogical and historical research. We also provide assistance for those interested in their family history."

The society's spring 2009 edition of *Panning for Nuggets of Old* is a wealth of information. In this ninety-four page book, it lists memory lane snippets, the history of the Parks Brothers Nursery and family genealogy tree, Claudie and Edna James, Mulberry Church of Christ founding, pictures and details about the George Wilson Store in Dean Springs, A.G. Benham family, Butterfield Stage route, deaths and burials in various cemeteries and so many things I won't list. These books are not expensive and would make treasured gifts for Christmas or birthdays. Some of the books for sale include: *History of Crawford County* by Clara B. Eno, *History in Headstones* by West & Swinburn, *Crawford County Marriages* by Oma Cole and Hazel Brown and *Ancestry Charts* from the Society members. The Society is nonprofit and money they receive is put back into the public as a service to you. It takes a lot of determined, dedicated people, working as a whole, to research and compile.

If you have wondered about your ancestors and don't know where or how to begin searching, all it takes is a phone call. The Society members know how to get you started and might have some material already accumulated. Open to the public, the Crawford County Genealogical Library can be accessed on Tuesday and Thursday and by appointment. Various family genealogies can be found in over 380 books. Other interesting county history and community information can be found on shelves. The Genealogical Library is located at 614 Fayetteville in Alma, Arkansas. Calendar year membership in the Crawford County Genealogical Society, Inc. is $20.00 for an individual and $21.00 for a couple. If you are interested, the members would be delighted to tell you the particulars. I learned the Society used to meet at Oma Cole's house in Dyer in 1972. Since her passing some ten years ago, their meetings were moved to the Alma Public Library. Imagine how much material has been laid before them ... all for Crawford County citizens and interested parties. Their time, work and generosity are what we receive. They are on key and opening the lock for us.

Yes, I did speak about how, when, where and why I began to write, about my parents and what they taught me. However, in the room sat years of knowledge–knowledge so flourishing I will never attain a portion of what they have amassed. Thank you very much for requesting me to attend. It was my privilege to share what I had to offer and learn from all of you.

I will pass along to you my closing remark. It was my mother's sage advice: "If you are in tune with yourself, you will never be off key."

PRIVATE TELEPHONE CONVERSATIONS
One-sided Conversations

Cell phones users have gone nuts. They are comical, astute, downright nasty, dangerous while driving and everything in between. There was a time when a telephone conversation was "private." You dialed out from the home, sat at the dining table to converse with your friend and sipped coffee at leisure. We didn't tote the phone as it was connected to a cord.

Then some brainiac invented cordless. It was a nice little contraption to place in the bathroom so you didn't have to jump out of the shower and slide from one end of the house on wet tile to answer the call. Larger than life cell phones came on the scene. They were all right but the battery made them top heavy. Enter cell phones so small, if you blink ... you might lose it. Everyone said they needed a cell phone for emergencies. It was a necessity because you couldn't afford to miss out on a conversation. If you were bogged down in the mud, someone was at your fingertips. Well, maybe, if you had a phone book in the car or numbers stored in the cell. Can't forget, though, if you are in a dead zone ... you might be among those using scratchy towels or in a room next to an ax wielding psycho. Gee whiz, don't drop it in a commode or sit on it because it will dial out to everyone and they will get the full impact from your latest meal.

Around Thanksgiving last year, a frantic lady was searching for a well known cooking guru's ingredients for a special dish. Whipping out her cell phone, her conversational tirade went something like this. "But, I need it. You don't understand. Without this special spice, it won't turn out right. I've been up and down the aisles twenty times and it's not here. What am I going to do?" She stared at me in desperation. "What would you do?" she said. Without thinking I said, "I don't have a clue because I don't cook Paula. I cook Joyce's and *Fort Smith Times Record*, Ms. Harshaw recipes. Why don't you phone Paula and tell her to come cook it?" She gave me a condescending look and huffed off.

Several weeks ago I was in Wal-Mart taking my time to read labels. Out of the corner of my eye, I saw a woman descending on me like a vulture out for road kill. I noticed her child was alone in the cart at the opposite end of the isle. She was speaking in a foreign language and nodding at me at the same time. I asked her what she said and she frowned. So much for conversation. Shrugging it off, I went about my business and entered another isle.

Well, bless my soul, she was at it again but this time, right in my face. Now, close proximity is not my forte and I am not especially fond of anyone six inches from my nose. I said, "Back up, lady. You are invading my space." She continued to talk and talk and talk and I didn't understand a word coming from her mouth. What's wrong with people? So help me, everywhere I went in Wal-Mart, she was behind me having a one sided conversation. When I reached the check-out, guess who was behind me? Yep, it was her and she was still talking. Had she not pushed her hair behind her ears, I would never have seen the small mouth piece attached to her ear.

The next week, I was doing my grocery shopping. Deep in thought, my brain was rattled when someone, a foot away from me, began spouting about an uncle having ingrown toenail surgery. I turned around thinking it was someone I knew. It wasn't. She continued to speak as loudly as she could about the whole family fighting over the commode from *Montezuma's Revenge*. She had a mess to clean when she went home. Brother Moses, why wait? Her conversation was not palatable. Thinking I was safe from more prattle, enter another well meaning soul with a cell phone. She was expanding the virtues of wiping the floor with her ex-husband and what a rotten son-of-a-bleep-bleep he was for telling her she was a slob. She expanded, "He never takes a bath and he calls me a slob!" It didn't stop there. Another was laughing like a hyena repeating verbatim the off color joke she had just been told.

I decided to check out. It wasn't so bad but being stuck between two people with cell phones plastered to the ear and jutting mouth pieces was almost too much. Conversations were in stereo, amped to the max. Everyone within a ten foot radius could hear one person say, "Hell, no, I haven't smoked for at least one day." Then a man giggled. "When are you going on vacation? Planning on getting a good tan? Be sure and wear the thong and let me see your naughty pictures." Holy mother of pearl this day was a Petri dish of grand proportions. I have heard about this, that or the other, who is being called to court, what you had for supper and who is getting divorced. Some are being sued, got a fine for speeding, had to buy head lice medicine and have fleas in their bed. One couple had a fight and she wound up with a black eye and her husband had a bloody nose. Bank accounts are overdrawn but you are writing a check anyway.

In an open "public" area, if another person can hear you converse on a cell phone, what you say aloud might not be considered "private." A lot of people may not like hearing your conversations but keep talking. I am taking mental notes. Who knows, I may be behind, next to or in front of you keeping my ears open for immense story lines and characters for a novel. If someone winks at you, smile. You may be in the next article of *Do You Remember*.

IN SOURCING vs. OUTSOURCING

There was a time and place, in the 20th century (not 21st), people did things for themselves. It didn't take a rocket scientist to figure out how to do menial jobs and we didn't hire out what should have been our duty. Forty some odd years ago a person was able to work on their own cars, bake things without using a microwave, and read a map. So many things have changed, it's impossible to do a task without drawing a schematic or hiring someone to do it. It's called outsourcing, a buzzing, dictating word that has changed American dreams and attitudes. Now the catchword is, "in-sourcing" meaning we do what we used to do but perhaps, better.

Before you have a thought of any "do it yourself" car repairs read your owner's manual. People used to do simple car repairs. You can't anymore without having a degree in mechanics because everything is computerized. The battery, in the majority of cars, used to be under the hood, easily reached to check its content, and jumper cables were in everyone's trunk. Not now. In some cars the battery is shoved under the back seat. Your passenger sits on top of the acid filled charger and you couldn't jump a stalled car even if you wanted to be a Samaritan filled with good tidings.

It takes two people to wedge themselves in the small backseat area, unhinge the seat, tug and pull it through the door or angle it upright to have room to work ... just to find the battery. Imagine going through all of that to secure jumper cables to start a motor. Attaching jumper cables to a new car battery is like blowing up an outhouse. You know you will be in a deep mess as the car might disintegrate to a melted down, crapped out computer unable to be booted. Jumper cables are useless but aren't a total loss ... that is, if you don't mind using them as a jumping rope. At least they have handles and with a little effort, give us a workout.

The little woman or stay at home mom baked with an honest to goodness oven without gigwhizzy computerized buttons. You know the kind. Gourmet meals, homemade bread, cookies for the kids and culinary delights were whipped up on it. It has four burners on top, can catch a skillet on fire and set off smoke alarms when you least expect it and was big enough for a twenty pound Thanksgiving turkey. It took a while to cook dinner meals but it was quality time. Enter the microwave oven and crafty gadgets with meals complete in ten minutes or less. No metal can be used within its interior, so out goes the old cast iron oven cookware. Go ahead; shove them in the back of the cabinet. The skillets won't care but to get even, they will rust.

Proud of the newfound small, I-don't-take-up-too-much-space, innovative quick cooking apparatus, you rush out to find the latest plastic cookware. You have to use microwave safe, not hot-to-touch containers so it doesn't explode and send you on a trip to Mars. Every kind of food can be cooked but you must read the manual or you will wind up with a rubberized piece of meat. Eggs will implode and make you search for a gas mask to keep from inhaling putrid sulfur. Any warmed over pizza tastes like cardboard, and atomic powered beans turn into fossilized rocks when zapped in the microwave. We don't have gizzards!

When you think you have mastered the "cooking inside out" heat seeking turnstile, it goes on a rampage and won't work. You can't fix it, so out it goes and in with the new. Don't forget, you have a surplus of cabinet crawling plastic ware containers but you have to buy different and better plastic. It's a waste to throw the old containers away, so, go ahead; cram them on top of the iron ware along with the washed margarine containers. Maybe the new containers won't melt or turn yucky with burned on, gag-me-with-a-spoon, food. What will it take to make us slow down, open up an old cookbook to prepare a family meal, use an ordinary stove with turn knobs and oven, and do "in-source" old-fashioned cooking?

I guess it really doesn't matter what we are accustomed to doing or if we hire someone to do things for us. We've gotten so used to all these new fandangle gadgets we'd be in a world of hurt if we had to deviate in order to live. What does matter is if we can count and not rely on a computer to tell us the sum or be able to read a map instead of relying on a GPS to locate our destination. As long as you know the sun comes up in the east and sets in the west, the western or eastern states shouldn't be too hard to find. If you are not traveling but going somewhere in your own town, buy a GPS as a portion of a street could be in the boondocks.

Why can't we "in-source" our own capabilities and use our minds, hands and muscle to provide for ourselves? The answer to this puzzle is called work.

Outsourcing provides jobs to a lot of people and without those jobs; our society would be at a complete standstill. There is nothing wrong with doing some "insourcing" for personal gratification. If you want a fast meal when you are traveling, need fast transportation in an emergency, have too many mouths to feed during Thanksgiving, need a doctor to set broken bones or something out of the ordinary, do what I do ... outsource.

KITES & MARCH WIND

Can you believe kites were available 2,800 years ago in China? Some kite authorities and authors of the subject say the kite was invented by Chinese philosophers, Mozi and Lu Ban of the fifth century. Their kite was made of paper and used as a source for some type of rescue mission. The earliest kites, they say, were flat and rectangular in form. Silk, one of China's industrial products was used as the cover and bamboo, prevalent in China, was the frame. All kinds of figures, dragons, pagodas, and drawings adorned the kite and were used in ceremonies. Kites were fashioned for kite fights and maneuvering the kite took skill as one opponent tried to cut the line of his foe. The kite took hold as it made its appearance in various parts of the world.

By 1750, Benjamin Franklin proposed to use the kite to prove lightning had electrical powers. Franklin may have flown a kite in Pennsylvania and caused electrical sparks to bounce from clouds but some theorized it didn't happen. It wasn't until 1752 that Thomas-Francois Dalibard proved Franklin's theory. Using a forty foot metal rod, Dalibard hoisted the rod into the air during a thunderstorm and sparks flew as the lightning struck the rod. Contrary to popular belief and according to Wikipedia, the free encyclopedia, a kite was not used and Franklin didn't jeopardize his life. He let Dalibard do the dangerous deed. Franklin, however, did invent lightning rods. Due to his discovery of electrical properties and burying metal rods attached to buildings or houses makes them safe. Thank goodness for his experiments or we all might go up in a puff of glory during electrical storms.

Modern day kites come in all shapes and sizes and colors and made of heavy material. The kite I tried to fly had a mind of its own, was made of flimsy paper and the sticks holding it together was made of balsa wood. With cellophane wound tightly round the kite, it appeared to be huge. Careful to extract the precious airborne contraption from its shell, I was anxious to see how the wind would lift it to the heavens. There was one little problem. I had to put the stupid thing together and didn't know beans from peas as to how it was done. Normally, instructions come with gadgets or a constructions diagram is attached. If I had learned to speak Chinese, I might have understood where "A" met "B." Unfolded, it laid in a heap as I stared at a tiny piece of string, two balsa wood sticks and a funny looking blob of paper.   Duh! How in Sam Hill would the paper stay on the cockeyed pieces of wood and where was the rest of the string? Better yet, where was the tail? Every kite I had seen had tons of string but this crazy kite wouldn't raise six inches off the ground. Putting my thinking cap on straight and rattling my pink matter, I realized the string slid inside elongated, glued down flaps on the edges of the paper. So much for that but where did the rest of the string attach? I was gritting my teeth because so far, this kite didn't resemble anything I had ever seen. Putting the two bars on the kite became a test of wills and I began to hate the horrid little patience tester.

SKIPPING DOWN MEMORY LANE

After a frustrating two hours and not telling anyone what I was doing, I marched to Mr. Matlock's grocery store and looked at him. I didn't say a word but the first words out of his mouth were, "Having a bit of trouble, aren't you? You should have waited till your daddy got off from work to put it together." Yes, I probably should have waited till Daddy guided my hands or gone next door to have the neighbor boys help me, but I was stubborn as a mule. I didn't want those sassy, know-it-all boys telling me I was a danged old girl and didn't have any business flying kites. What did they know?

After listening to Mr. Matlock go through all the ins and outs and this and thats, I decided to unhinge the thing and let Daddy help me. It's a good thing because the kite, left to my construction, would have flown backward and whacked someone in the head. It was one of a kind. Oddly, the tail I floundered with appeared with a scissor and old shirt and the non-existent string magically popped out of Daddy's pocket. I watched Daddy's hands put it together in less than fifteen minutes and with a little finesse it was soaring up, up, up in the air until all the string uncoiled. It was my turn to fly the beauty and Daddy tied the string around my wrist. The power of the March wind and kite nearly pulled me upward. As the kite tugged to go further in the sky and did die-does in various directions, I could feel the string cut into my wrist. Why on earth I wanted to fly a kite ... didn't make sense. Had Daddy not been standing close to me, I would be somewhere in the wild blue yonder playing pat-a-cake with the man in the moon and I sure as heck wouldn't be writing this story.

JOYCE RAPIER

Everyone reading this story about kites has probably had an experience in flying a box, triangular, oval or octagon shaped kite and memories to match. You've extracted them from trees, snapped the frames and taped them together, watched as they coiled around electric wires and stomped the ground when the wind stole your favorite kite. Contests with your friends to see how much higher your kite would go, is no longer important. You've sworn never to buy another one but at the same time, watched and pointed when you saw a kite in the sky. Now days, kites don't seem to have the hold on a child. Little feet don't run with the wind on a March day nor do children lie on grassy mounds as they daydream of mastering the will of a kite.

You can quote me on this. Wind and kites are partners but a memory ropes the kite and tames the wind.

BLUE LAW

Blue law was, by definition, "no sales" on Sunday. I can remember when all stores in Van Buren shut down tighter than a tick on a hound dog in observance of Sunday. In Arkansas, it meant no sales of any "intoxicating alcoholic liquors" and in general, to uphold this law, all stores were locked. No last minute shopping because you forgot a quart of milk and if your bread was stale, you ate it. If your stove blew up or your refrigerator went on the fritz, you were out of luck. I am telling you, if you didn't buy it on Saturday, tough luck. There was no way of buying anything unless someone took pity on your soul, broke the law to help you get what you needed and told you to keep your mouth shut. In their way of thinking, it was your word against theirs.

Blue law was a moral issue. Morality can't be legislated because if it were, everyone would be thrown in the clinker for doing the minutest thing, if it didn't agree with law. There would be a jail on every corner. Certain laws or rules, set forth by the early settlers in the 1600's, were to enforce good morals on immoral souls. It was a Puritanical way to insure the Sabbath would be a total day of rest and to keep the peace. These persons maintained giving food to heretics or Quakers, walking in certain places or giving any child affection was against their rules. If you didn't adhere to strict obedience, you would be chastised.

In the eighteenth century, when the temperance movement was in full force, "blue" was in reference to

79

'bluenoses' or those persons whose strict puritanical beliefs defied those who believed otherwise. New England states had their own definition of blue law in what people could do and not do. The Blue Law, (supposedly written on blue paper ... can't be established as fact), is still in effect in many states, regulating sales of automobiles, alcoholic beverages, house wares and other types of goods because it's easier to keep the laws intact than try to erase them.

Many blue laws in the state of Arkansas were repealed in 1957. The laws bounced around until 1982 when the Arkansas Supreme Court struck down Act 135. Although Arkansas Code does not have blue laws, city councils or directors have authority to create ordinances. Today, some stores never close their doors as they are open 24/7 for last minute shoppers. Holidays, for some establishments, do not exist as their every movement revolves around providing goods to buyers. However, fourteen states (including Arkansas) still exist with the "blue law" movement but they apply to "spirits." Those restaurants or hotels that have a permit are allowed on-premises drinks, providing the area is in a jurisdiction voted for legal Sunday sales. Maybe it's a double standard, but then again, I don't drink. It won't concern me unless some over the limit drinker decides to do me bodily harm. The hours for purchase /consumption vary in different states.

Hunting is banned on Sunday in some states. To this day, there are states that cannot sell or trade automobiles on Sunday, except those who worship Sabbath from sunset Friday to sunset Saturday. From the 1600's until now, you would think our laws wouldn't be so archaic. I guess it really doesn't matter because when one law changes another takes its place.

SKIPPING DOWN MEMORY LANE

Sometimes changing a law makes it worse than sticking to the original.

What will happen when every shopper decides to surf the internet for the latest fashion, books, shoes or appliances? You can find most anything on e-bay, whether it's used or new, including automobiles. Trouble is, using this form of shopping; someone may take you for a joy ride you didn't want to enjoy. Caveat emptor! Scan Amazon and most anything you wish to purchase is in front of your face, including cosmetics. Before you decide to purchase a jar of one ounce skin cream via the internet, measure out one ounce and see how little it is. You may be spending more than you anticipate.

Nearly every manufacturer of major appliances has a website. If it's out there, you can find it. There is no gasoline involved, hunting a parking space or taking a chance with a virus lurking on push carts. Everything on-line that you purchase is delivered to your door. Sure, you may pay delivery charges and taxes, but for the most part, it might average out in comparison to your miles per gallon.

Those seeking alcoholic beverages can find their choice of drink on the web. They better order it during the week to have it in hand before Sunday. The way sales on the internet have "coupon" catches for luxury items and clothing, it will soon be the way to shop. If internet shopping is the new wave of the future, what will happen to all the remaining Blue laws still on the books? Will all those laws be enforced if people do their shopping via the internet? Will we be scrutinized, chastised, or victimized by our choices? If so, it means all our freedoms to purchase internet valuables or frivolous whims will be subject to someone looking over our shoulders telling us we broke a law. Regardless of how, where, or when we purchase items, some Blue laws, enacted in the 1600's will remain. I suppose, since its five centuries later, we will forever be under its juris-"prude"nce.

If you purchase via the internet, one thing you won't have is the luxury of having hands on or viewing something in person. You might as well forget camaraderie, smiles and laughter with people you like to visit with at your local store. Personally, I enjoy visiting with people. In fact, I visit more than I shop because I know a Blue law cannot squelch my freedom of speech. Oops! Freedom of speech (first amendment) may not come under the header of "blue" law, but yep, you guessed it … there are laws prohibiting some types of speech. In order to stay in line with the "blue" law, I best go find a bonnet, pantaloons, knee high clogs, front to back apron, and old fashioned floor to neck dress to keep me in fashion with the 1600's. While I am at it, I better plaster a new fandangle band-aid over my mouth because we all know freedom of speech ends where the other guy's nose begins. We only think we live in the 21st Century! Our 1600 year ancestors are dead as a hammer but somehow, some of their piranha, clamp jawed, Blue laws still tell us what, where, how and when we can purchase things. Good grief!

Read:
http://encyclopediaofarkansas.net/encyclopedia/entry-detail.aspx?entryID=4298 for details.

If you want to read the whole shebang, go to http://en.wikipedia.org/wiki/Blue_law.

THE OLD TWO LANE BRIDGE

Some of you will remember the old two lane bridge connecting Van Buren to Fort Smith and others will probably say, "Who cares?" Most of us enjoy a glimpse of the past as it unites the future in how quickly the years fade away.

The silver span was, at best, a scary proposition. Not because it was a bridge, but knowing the automobiles could, at any moment, plow into one another. There were quite a few cars in the 50's & 60's and they were large and made out of metal, not fiberglass or plastic. Depending on what kind of "soup job" was under the hood hinged on how quickly it sped.

My dad had one of those "souped-up" cars and delighted in scaring the beejeebers out of anyone willing to sit in the passenger seat. There were no "oh hell handles" to grasp or seat belts to anchor a body to the scratchy seats. You might cover your face with your hands, say a little prayer to get home safely, and then kiss the ground when you exited the car. Daddy was a speed demon, fed on gasoline and with his heavy foot on the gas pedal, it maxed out the carburetor. I think he secretly wanted to race cars because we went to all the dust and rock flying exhibitions, especially the one at the curve on Wild Cat Mountain Road in Fort Smith.

Getting back to the bridge, here's how it plays. It was not uncommon to have a back log of cars wait for hours when a car broke down or had a wreck on the bridge. Believe me; it happened more often than not and sitting in the middle of the bridge, feeling the water pound the supports didn't make me a happy camper. Entrances for the Van Buren side was either over the viaduct to enter Van Buren using highways 64-71 going east on Broadway, or by using the egress toward the ice plant. Going over the viaduct, people turning right toward Broadway didn't have to stop unless a driver intended to turn left toward the Crawford County Courthouse. Then it was screeching tires, a few choice words or a loud, scrunching bang. Both areas, in my opinion, were for going around the corner on two wheels, angled on the side and praying for divine intervention.

This was before the "fast lane" or aptly called, emergency vehicle pass. The lane was not meant for passenger cars, but everyone used it. The lane was narrow, barely wide enough to keep the fenders or running boards from scraping the rails, and then merged into the two-lane viaduct above the Missouri Pacific Railroad tracks. People raced like the devil was on their heels to see which car could go over the bridge first and laid on the horn to make sure someone else knew you were coming. It sounded like a herd of hollowed out cow horns blaring "get out of my way; you're not branding my backside."

I remember one time Daddy decided to take the fast lane. As he looked in the rear view mirror, an ambulance was fast approaching the bumper of our car. His foot hit the accelerator and we shot down the lane like a bottle rocket. He didn't put on the brakes when he neared the merge, and Mother nearly had a heart attack. However, the ambulance continued to dog Daddy. Faster than a speeding bullet, over the viaduct we went, sped around the corner on two wheels, continued around another corner to Broadway and out through East End. Did Daddy slow down? No! When we reached Gracelawn Cemetery on the narrow, curvy two-lane highway, a state trooper took the lead. Sirens were screaming, cars were honking like mad to avert a major disaster, and people were running out of the small motels to find out what was happening.

Mother's hair was standing on end, but Daddy didn't bat an eyelid. My sister, Hazel, and I were in the floorboard scared out of our wits. Daddy worked as a Carmen Inspector for the Missouri Pacific Railroad, but this time in history, was also a constable for the City of Van Buren. His duties as a constable were not those of an actual sheriff or police officer but he wore his badge with pride, and felt it was his duty to go wherever danger led him. I wanted to yell. "Let me out of the car. You can do it on your own." but I didn't. He let the ambulance pass and followed it to its destination.

You've heard the old tune and probably sang these words. "Over the river and through the woods, to grandmother's house we go." Well, by golly, we went over the river but didn't go to Grandma's house. We wound up in the woods at Mountainburg by ripping around the hair pin curves, passing everything in sight, and dodging those cars coming up the treacherous, two lane mountain.

I was glad to see the old bridge go by the wayside, but at the same time, felt a little sad. Not for the bridge, mind you, but for my dad as it was time for him to let go of another season of his youth.

LOST AND FOUND

Last Sunday as I sat here going through the first edits of my book, the doorbell rang. A young boy stood there with a MinPin. The MinPin was a beautiful little thing and friendly as friendly could get. "Is this your dog?" My answer was no. He told me the tiny dog jumped inside their car.

I suppose being lost would make anyone or anything try to find safety. My first instinct was to tell him to phone the radio station but it was Sunday and the radio programs are pre-recorded. Phoning the newspaper wouldn't have helped because it would take a couple of days to see an ad posted. His mother waited in the car as he told me the story. As he started to go down the street to the neighboring houses, we told him they didn't have dogs. The dog probably lived closer to where his house was located. Seeing this small child with a lost dog on a leash, rattle my senses. I wanted to sweep the dog up in my arms and cry with him. It brought back memories in living color.

All day long I worried about the dog, the person to whom he belonged and if he would be reunited with the ones he loved. I could sense the desperation in the heart of the owner ... visualize them pacing the floor and calling his name. When Dan went to the store, he saw an officer with the Van Buren Pound. He watched him place a small dog inside the unit's metal cage. Perhaps the tiny, four-legged, sad eyed pet would be reunited with its owner. Each day, I read the lost and found section of the newspaper.

On Thursday morning, an ad appeared. At 7:00 in the morning I dialed the number but got a recording. No sooner had I sat down to drink my coffee, the phone rang. I proceeded to tell the lady about the little dog, the young boy and the dog catcher. It was strange, I thought, the little dog managed to travel so far from a house behind Wal-Mart and how the little dog wound up in Vista Hills. She told me she thought the MinPin belonged to a dear friend of hers and that her friend's dog, Chuckie, disappeared while the lady was having tests run at the hospital. Somehow the dog squeezed through her friend's fenced yard and escaped. Chuckie, the little MinPin, was her whole life and brought happiness to her. She was devastated and worried sick.

I wished her a Merry Christmas and told her I hoped the MinPin was her friend's dog. I asked her to keep me posted. The afternoon, on Christmas Eve, brought some sad news. It appeared the MinPin the dog catcher retrieved was claimed by a person on Mount Vista. I was glad the MinPin was found and reunited with its owner but sad the lady would still be in a state of anguish. I hope and pray she finds her Chuckie.

My insides burned as if I had eaten a pile of hot coals. Tears welled up in my eyes as I knew, first hand, the desperation the owner of the lost dog was feeling. When I was around six years old, we had a Manchester terrier named Rowdy. He sired a litter of puppies with another Manchester terrier. They were pure bred. I wouldn't let Daddy select any dog but the one I wanted. It was futile for Daddy to protest. Our new puppy was unusual in that most Manchester's have short hair but Meanness's hair was silky and flowed like Angel hair in the breeze. He was beautiful and captured my heart. We were inseparable until one horrible day.

The day started off with a swimming outing at Cedar Creek in Figure Five. We were having a wonderful time, floating on inner tubes and throwing sticks for Rowdy and Meanness to retrieve. Meanness was a nosy little dog, ornery as sin and meaner than a rattle snake. He would attack anyone who got around me. It's why his name became Meanness. When we looked up, he was gone and so was Rowdy. Rowdy returned when we called his name but Meanness didn't return. He was somewhere in the woods at Figure Five.

For hours Daddy searched the area but there was no sign of him. It was getting dark and we had to go home. Daddy had to pick me up and forcefully put me in the car because I was determined to traipse all over the woods to find my dog. In major protest, we went home. That night and consecutive three week nights, I cried myself to sleep. Every day after work, Daddy would take me back and we would look some more. We went to every house in Figure Five to tell them about Meanness and gave our telephone number to those who had phones.

Food didn't taste good and playing was not the same ... I didn't have Meanness to sit up and beg for food or chase me around our fenced yard. I kept hearing Mother tell Daddy, "J.D. we need to find Meanness or get another dog before she wastes away to nothing." My life was in chaos, my heart split apart and I didn't want another dog. I wanted Meanness so I prayed. I didn't know if God heard me or if, Daddy told me, God sometimes says, "No. It's a lesson learned." I resigned to the hard, cruel fact, Meanness may never come home.

Daddy knew I liked to go with him to the Van Buren Feed Store to look at the newly hatched chicks in their incubators and pet the bunny rabbits. Reluctantly, I went with him, protesting with all my might as I wanted to stay near the telephone. What if someone called us to tell they found Meanness? We wouldn't be home!

We had been at the store for an hour and I was desperate to go back home. Then the most wonderful thing happened. A man who lived in Figure Five waltzed through the door with a scraggly, matted hair, skinny dog that appeared near death. He told Daddy the dog nearly took his hand off when he tried to capture him and resisted any kind of coaxing. The man said he watched the little dog grab a bite of scrap food and run back to his barn. For three weeks, it was the same scenario. When he spoke to other people in the area, he realized who owned him. In desperation, he threw a sheet around him and put him in a box. The poor little dog was emaciated but still breathing.

When the dog saw me and I saw him, I screamed to high heaven. As weak as he was, he leapt from the man's arms and came directly to me. It was Meanness … my little lost dog.

SNIPE HUNTING

It's pitch black outside and the lumps in the throat grow larger. Fear is gripping you and you know if you don't catch one of the elusive critters, you won't be indoctrinated into the group. You are thinking ... it's the pits moving to this new area. I'm in Van Buren and I am alone with no friends. My friends are back in the old town I left. How I wish I could still be among them but alas, the parents needed to move forward and I with them. New school chums are smart and wily in ways I never expected. They seem friendly enough but are still at arm's length. The teachers seem aloof to the desperation clinging inside my guts but, they are teachers. What can I expect, they don't know me as a person but I need to show them I am adept in achieving greatness. A sudden movement in the trees brings you back to the present. What was that awful noise? Was it behind me or in front of me? I can't tell its direction. Which way am I facing? I was told to stand with my face to the north but I have moved too many times to know which direction is north. You have to get this right.

It was a dastardly and sometimes dangerous prank for those new to an area but those pulling the joke thought it was hilarious. A group of kids (usually boys) would haze the new kid on the block. Most times, on school grounds, the boys would be in their usual clique. They would be whispering when the new kid approached. Sometimes shy, the new person would ask what was going on as he wanted to fit into the group. The boys would shuffle their feet as a gesture of hem-hawing around knowing they would be pumped for information. After a few minutes of trying to dissuade the new kid from learning the secret, one of them would pull him aside and tell him about the great snipe hunt. It wouldn't be easy but if he could catch one of the snipes he would be part of the snipe troupe. Was he in or out, the choice was his. Naturally, he thought he was macho so, in order to show his prowess, he said yes.

The date was set. They would meet when it got dark and drive to a well known secluded spot. The boy must wear something dark so he wouldn't be seen by the snipes. Any exposed skin had to be covered with black or brown paste shoe polish. The snipes had keen eyes and enormous sense of smell so be sure to mask the human scent. You must rub some type of camphor liniment on the skin as it thwarted the snipe's ability to judge human approach. The scent of camphor mimicked the pheromone of a snipe. All of these things were supposed to pull a snipe's sense of smell and direction toward the capturer.

The gear to catch the snipe was a burlap bag, two sticks or large rocks and a long piece of string to tie the top of the burlap bag closed. The snipe must not escape as it could chew the arm off. The kid wanted to know what a snipe looked like. Was it large with fangs or claws? Did it climb trees or hide under rocks? We can't tell you that secret, it will be up to you to find out on your own. How do you catch one of these critters? Why the sticks and rocks? Do you hit it in the head with the rock or jab it with a stick? He was told to whack the sticks or rocks together while making an awful sound with the throat. The click of sticks or rocks was a mating signal of snipes and the sound of the human throat (sort of a gurgle) was the acceptance noise.

After an hour of hiding, watching and listening to the kid whack the noise makers, the boys lurking in the woods or near a stream of water, would come toward the kid and tell him the snipes moved to another place. Loading up in the car, they resumed their travel to another place. More thwacking and gurgling didn't find a snipe. It was time to go home. You were lucky if they drove you home. Sometimes a kid was stranded in the woods all night long as the "supposed" friends abandoned him. Naturally, the kid was devastated not catching a snipe as it meant he wouldn't become a member of the snipe troupe.

The next day at school, the boy, whose face and hands were slathered with black or brown shoe paste, was noticed. Most of the shoe polish still adhered to the skin and everyone knew he was a victim of snipe hazing. Some kids laughed knowing he was so gullible but the snipe troupe hoisted him on their shoulders and pranced around with the kid brave enough to manhandle the snipe hunt. He was now considered part of the group as he passed the test of enduring the dark of night and imaginary creatures. The "egg" on his face faded.

In our area, it was a fantasy task, a wild goose chase of a non-existent critter. This form of hazing went out of fashion as kids got wise to the idiocy of snipe hunting. Many forms of jokes or pranks to indoctrinate newcomers still exist but most people are smart enough to figure it out before they become the brunt of its insanity. What is apropos to snipe hunting is

SKIPPING DOWN MEMORY LANE

there is a shore bird called the common snipe. The shorebird is extremely difficult for experienced hunters to trap or kill. Way back in 1770, if a British Indian soldier killed a snipe (bird) they were considered snipers. For all of those easy to fleece kids prancing around in the woods, who didn't catch a snipe, you played the part. Camouflage, stealth engaged for combat you may not have captured a phantom snipe but you did succeed. You may have only "scoped" for the snipe in our neck of the woods but you dressed the part as a "sniper" in military terminology. To all the pranksters pulling the joke on your peer prey, you were ambushed ... the "yolk" is on you!

ANTLION & DOODLEBUG

When I was small, I would run through tall Johnson grass at the bottom of our yard. It abutted the narrow alleyway on the east of our property. On the fence, in that area, grew honeysuckle vines. Those two, wild growing, invasive plants nearly drove Daddy nuts. The yellow honeysuckle grew so fast, it nearly bent the wire fence out of commission. The Johnson grass was almost impossible to extract when the roots began putting out runners. Because both these plants survive over winter, the growth cycle never stopped. They were merely stunted.

Three months before it was time to put in the garden on this flat area of our yard, Daddy sprayed diesel fuel on the fence and ground. It stunk to high heaven but the worst part was that I no longer could run through the dried grass or watch for the aromatic honeysuckle to bloom. I loved to traipse down to the garden area because it's where I could watch the doodlebugs or roly-poly. More often than not, I usually took a mason jar and collected tons of the little bugs that rolled up in a ball when on the defensive.

They reminded me of an Armadillo because their exterior shell appeared armor coated. They are an isopod called *Armadillium Vulgare*. I have no clue as to what the bugs are good for except for little kids to be amazed when all those legs curl inside a ball. When it was time for Daddy to burn the grass and vine, I sang a song I created. *Doodlebug, doodlebug, you better not laze. Daddy's got matches to make a blaze. You best be a moving cause you're liable to scorch. Oops, I tried to tell you but you done been torched.*

Near our stoop, where Daddy piled a truck load of sand to mix with Portland cement to complete our front porch, the remaining residue of sand made the soil soft and pliable. It was cool beneath bare feet and swished between toes. It almost felt like a soft talcum powder. It wasn't like the red clay on the south side of our house where if you stepped in it when it was wet, it took a chisel to scrape it from the shoes. Every morning a mysterious sight appeared in the sand. It captivated me to no end and as I watched the activity around it, it mystified me.

A single file of ants made their way near the area, scurrying about as if their world was about to end. In a sense, it was. If I blinked, an ant disappeared. Hard as I tried to keep from blinking, I never could figure out why the disappearing ant escaped my sight. One after the other, an ant was being sucked into an abyss, a vacuum of sorts, right in front of me.

What were these strange looking holes? They reminded me of perfect dunce hats, only they were inverted. The point end was about one half inch beneath the surface while the round, larger circumference was almost one inch across. The cones never had a grain of sand disturbed even when an ant fell into the valley. At one point, I laid on my stomach to watch what was happening but never saw anything. I was astounded. Was it an actual phenomenon or something my mind created? I had about all I could stand. Every day it was the same thing but come hell or high water, I would find out where all those ants were going.

Mother warned me not to keep picking up strange bugs and not to drag them into the house. Somehow, I turned a deaf ear and this day would be no different. Marching into the house I told Mother I needed a big spoon. Of course, she wanted to know why I felt the need to take another spoon outside. She handed me a spoon and told me this time to bring it back inside the house. She muttered something about all her spoons disappearing. The last thing I heard was "picking a switch off the tree" if I didn't mind her. With the spoon in hand, I was determined to catch some kind of bug or critter. To heck with the switch, I wanted to find out what was making all those holes. Besides, she only switched me one time. I remembered the sting and also, stripping all the fine limber branches on the tree. There was nothing to pick.

Back down on my stomach, I watched as an ant fell into the hole and the spoon was in hot pursuit. Using my right hand, I dug as deep as I could and what I pulled out of that hole scared me senseless. As I flicked up a mound of the sand, out popped a weird tiny bug with pinchers. The bug and portions of ants landed in my left hand. The bug was not large but about the size of a pinky fingernail. It was light tan with specks of dark brown on the top side of its body but the pinchers were huge.

I let out a blood curdling scream and Mother came running. She was as white as a sheet thinking I was dying. When I showed her what I had in my hand she told me it was an antlion larva. The antlion, depending on its hungriness, makes small or large holes in soft soil. A larva goes backward in the soft soil making a circle. Then using its head it flips the soil upward leaving its head buried just beneath the soil, pinchers up ready to strike. When an ant slips into the cone, it pinches and eats it.

All of this was brought to mind when I was cleaning off my front porch. There, in the soft soil beneath a Laurel bush, were several perfectly shaped upside down dunce hats. I knew what they were and why they were there. I had some hungry antlions. No, I didn't go get a spoon from my kitchen because if I did, I would have to pick a switch.

FISHIN' & GIGGIN'

When I was small, Grandma and Grandpa Hawkins lived at the top of Knox Street. The Lingo's were their neighbor and Mr. Lingo and Grandpa always went fishing. I often thought they were born with a fishin' pole or gig in their hands. The Arkansas River was close to the houses. In fact, a body could almost spit off a porch into the water. Right at the curve at the top of Knox, there was a horse pasture and lean-to for the critters. The north side of the lean-to had several large nails driven into a large plywood board. Those nails were used to hold catfish heads and body in place as they skinned the fish. Bass and other fish were laid on a wood plank anchored to homemade saw horses. Stinky old fish scales were plenty.

To get to the river, Mr. Lingo and Grandpa had a well worn path to the river's edge. The path included going down steep rocky areas as the river was below the bluff. Below the bluff, the sand bank formed a natural jetty from sediment when it rained. At this point, they might use a small flat bottomed boat to throw out a seine or fish from the bank. It depended on the weather and temperature of the water whether they brought home fish. Using a seine to catch fish was something everyone did back then as it was not illegal and you didn't have to worry about weather forecasts. If a seine was used, they kept only the largest fish and threw back all the others. Most times though, they were after catfish bottom feeders and it might take all day to catch one fish. On the river bank, they rigged up areas where the fishing pole could be stuck securely in the sand so they could walk away and fish other areas. When the tip of the pole bent nearly into the water, they knew a catfish was on the line. Grandpa said they were sneaky, in that they sometimes nibbled on dough/liver balls and left him the hook. If he was really unlucky, the fish would take hook, line, swivel and sinker and sometimes pole into the water. That is what happened one day and Grandpa swore by heaven and earth; the fish had to be as large as the flat bottomed boat and he would catch that fish if he had to go under water to snag him.

It took several weeks before Grandpa and Mr. Lingo's luck paid off. Grandpa had rigged up a three pronged circle hook. Actually, it was three circle hooks wired together making it look like a boat anchor. He said if he couldn't get that fish on one circle the other two might do the trick. When the whooping and hollering could be heard for miles around, you knew they hit pay dirt.

The fish was a flathead whopper ... almost the size of the flat bottom boat and nearly 200 pounds. That cat had to be in the river for years gulping down every fish in its sight. For them to haul the cat back up the path and through the boulders, they had put it on gunny sacks and tie a rope inside its mouth and around the body. When they got the fish up to the lean-to they were so out of breath they could barely talk. To top it off, none of the nails on the shed could hold it upright without pulling the shed to the ground. What were they to do? The homemade saw horses couldn't handle the fish as they would have snapped like match sticks. They slung a rope over a large tree limb and hoisted the humongous fish off the ground. They were so proud of that catfish it's all they talked about for weeks...the one that didn't get away.

Going giggin' was another story and I am here to tell you that it was no picnic. Giggin' had to be done at night, preferably during the spring as the bullfrogs greedeeped their mating calls. The best place to catch a large bullfrog was at the river's edge or near a brushy embankment. I wasn't very old but I do remember sitting near a campfire on the Arkansas River and swatting mosquitoes. It seemed like the whole family traipsed on this outing as my mom, dad, sister, cousins, their parents and grandparents thought it was the best thing since sliced bread.

We kids were doing things kids do, scream, laugh and fight. Every now and then, the adults would rein us in telling us we had to be quiet to gig frogs or fish. How boring as I sure had no desire to eat a frog, let alone have one pee on me and they couldn't persuade me a fish could hear what I was saying or doing. It was a standoff with my hands on my hips telling Daddy he might as well take me home. Daddy kept telling me frog legs taste like chicken and I was adamant telling him ... I'll eat the fish but I ain't a eatin' one of them slimy bull froggie things. When we realized the adults were serious everyone got quiet. It was time to gig.

The gig was a small, three tined pitchfork attached to a long bamboo handle with a long piece of rope. When the gig was thrown, the rope was what Daddy used to pull back the gig and frog. Daddy had a strap secured carbide lamp that he attached to his head as it helped keep his hands free when he was giggin'. The carbide lamp or flashlight was a necessity as a light, shined in a frog's eyes, kept them from seeing a person advance. Bad thing though, it also drew snakes.

As usual, Daddy toted a pistol on his hip and a derringer in his pocket ... just in case! For what? Kablooie, a 45 caliber shot rang out in the night air. People were screaming bloody hell and Mother asked, with a few choice blue words, what he thought he was doing. "Cille, look down at your feet." There was a hole in the sand bar about the size of a cannon ball and bits and pieces of a water moccasin lay scattered all over the place. The rest of the night I sat in one place, near the campfire, watching and listening for the next shot. I told Daddy if he would take me home he could have the money I saved from the tooth fairy to buy some frog legs. I crossed my heart and hoped to spit I would eat the whole frog.

Events of that night were those I would never forget. If it wasn't female mosquitoes slurping blood out of me, it was poisonous snakes being blown to smithereens. I don't think I ever heard so many pistol shots in one night or saw so many holes in a sand jetty. Fishin' and giggin' on that crazy evening was lucrative as they caught a passel of fish and several bull frogs to feed all of us. Another thing I won't forget is watching Mother cook those blasted frog legs and watching something dead try to leap out of the frying pan because the tendons weren't clipped. Next on the unforgettable list was having Daddy get the last laugh as I found out those old frogs weren't slimy and tasted like chicken. Last and most important for all of those of you who ask. Yes, I will eat frog legs but don't ask me to go ... I ain't giggin'!

JOYCE RAPIER

GIVE ME A LIVE BODY!

Do you remember a time and place when a receptionist answered the phone? She might say, "XYZ Tumblebug Service" but by golly, she was a live person. You couldn't see her face but the lilt to her voice meant she was doing a service / job by answering the phone. There was no, "hold please, hold please" while you waited ten minutes for her to return to your call. You were important to their company and it meant they valued you as a customer.

The other day I phoned a company to purchase a product. It was an exasperating, monumental experience and like me, I am sure you have heard the same thing. When it sounds like a live body is answering a phone and you take a breath to reply, you gulp down the urge to speak. "Listen closely as our menu has changed," was given in English and then WHAM, it was repeated in Spanish. Ninety miles a minute this person rattles out a list of options with canned, nasal, monotone sputtering and never once do you hear what you want to hear. "If you know your party's extension, you may dial it at any time during this menu."

Ok, I don't know the number so I wait for another dumb minute before the list continues. "If you want to reference an account number, please say "two." If you don't know the account numbers say "three." I am mute as I don't have an account number. "I didn't get a correct answer. I will repeat the option," she goes on to say. While she is speaking, I automatically spit out a few words she does not understand. She repeats the same danged thing and then the line goes dead. She disappears into thin air. This time, I punch the telephone number with total disgust and reconnect with the same idiotic line of questioning. However, this time the menu is different. I don't know what I punched on the telephone because I was livid but I do know it was not the original number. Somehow, I do believe I reached someone in India! I couldn't understand a word this person spoke because there was a major language barrier. I slammed down the phone.

One by one, the telephone number was methodically punched to make certain I dialed the right number. Smoke was shooting out of my ears and I was gritting my teeth. All I wanted was a live body to answer the phone! No way will it happen as there is no such person. They are all dead and buried under menus. This time, I have to wait in line as my call will be answered according to a call waiting list. It won't take more than five minutes. I listen, impatiently, to a long repeated tirade of web addresses and music louder than a tympani orchestra. Twelve minutes later, the music is still blaring. My ear is sore but I know we are still connected. I lay down the phone and wait.

Four minutes later, it's now sixteen minutes into the call, eleven minutes more than I was told. I refuse to hang up the phone as the waiting list will grow longer. It's quite apparent to me; many people are having the same trouble because they want to talk to a live body. The music stopped and I jerked up the phone. A menu began. "If you know your party's extension line, you may dial it at any time during this menu. If you wish to enter your account number, punch two at this time. If you know your party's last name punch three, as it's alphabetically programmed and will direct you to their extension line. Dial four if you wish to disconnect." What? How asinine. The recording continued. "Dial five to repeat this menu. If you wish to speak to a customer service representative, dial number one."

Why in the name of sweet petunias did they not say number one in the first place and forget all the other numbers? I punch number one and wait and wait and wait and wait. Geesh Louise, it's now thirty minutes later and I still haven't talked to a live body. As I live and breathe, this cockeyed, supposedly live person is out to lunch and I get a recording. "You have reached Blah Blah's voice mail. So sorry I can't come to the phone. If you will leave a message, I will return it in the order it was received. Please leave a brief message to the order of this call referencing your account number and a telephone number where you may be reached. Due to the excessive messages I receive, it may be later this afternoon before I return your call."

Grrrr! What a waste of my time as they surely didn't need my business. Much later in the afternoon, I recognized the incoming call. It was from the company I dialed. To be a snit, I decided to do a bit of reciprocating. Very nasal, I said, "The number you have dialed is not a working number. If you feel this is in error, please hang up and dial your number again." I hung up the phone and sure enough, my phone rang again ... it was the same caller.

"Allo," I said with a sugar tone weird accent. Telling me who she was, I replied. "My name is Helga. I am from Zaveeden and I sorry, my Englai be broken. Nah, nah, she die. She not here. She hold too long and die from z'call menu list." There was dead silence on the phone and then I heard her scream, "Oh, my God!" I hung up the phone, did a high five with imaginary Helga, and swore never to use their services. If a company puts me on hold for thirty minutes and then switches me to a recording because they can, it means they don't have time for me and they don't need my money.

I know things have changed since telephone service added all their bells and whistles to "save money" by eliminating harried receptionists but it has gone too far. Having a home answering machine is almost a necessity when both spouses work, but a company needing business to survive ... I have news for you. You are losing money because of your canned menus. One of these days, I hope companies will realize what a disservice they are doing to the public with "hold please" and "listen closely as our menu has changed." Maybe they will do the wakeup call, smell their coffee burning before they go bankrupt, and realize ... the public wants a live body.

I AM NOT ELLIE MAE CLAMPETT

Mother had this thing for critters. If she saw a stray beside the road she would bring it home. If a critter was hungry Mother fed it. Daddy could dip it in creosote if it had mange, fleas or ticks. Quite a few times we saw dogs run like the devil was after them because one dip in the coal tar either cured or killed them. Daddy always had gallons of creosote on hand because it was used in preserving railroad cross ties. The color of it is amber to almost black and we never knew if a white dog would come out of the dip as a black or reddish yellow. Whatever color they emerged, you can bet your bottom dollar, they would howl at the moon because of the stinging sensation.

Since Daddy raised beagles, he knew what to do to get the dogs on the mend. At the time, the city didn't enact mandatory rabies or city tags but Daddy would vaccine them anyway. He would go to the Van Buren Feed Store, purchase vials and keep them on hand for Mother's emergency critter find. Every dog or cat Mother rescued was given rabies shots and fed until they were well enough to be adopted out. At one time, I do believe we had twenty-one cats and fifteen dogs running loose on our fenced plot of land. It wasn't only dogs and cats taking up residence at our house but other critters that Mother rescued. I'm not using the term "critters" lightly as we never knew what would craw, jump, fly or bite. The first, in a long line-up, was a hawk. It wasn't a wimpy little bird but one with talons the size of a meat hook. Mother and Daddy on one of their excursions to the wild found it on the side of the road. Its wing was broken. Naturally, Mother with her "I've got to fix this critter" brought it home. Bad, bad mistake. When they got home Daddy exited the car with a frown on his face. That wasn't all he had. He looked as though he had a fight with a tiger. Jagged, bloody gouges pitted his arm and his face was peppered with wing scrapes. I don't know how he managed to fix the hawk's wing but he did. He named it Mr. Talon. Daddy kept the hawk in a large pen and fed it field mice. Any cat that ventured too close to the cage was history. Several weeks later and many more boxing matches with the hawk, Daddy released it back to the wild. Thank God and greyhound that bird was gone!

We had a torrential downpour and the river was near flood level. Water was flooding the low areas and all the areas for critters to be safe were in jeopardy. Enter two skunks. One was a female, the other male. They were tiny little babies when Mother and Daddy found them near the levee. The mother skunk was no where around so Mother picked up the kits and brought them home. In order to keep the scent from overpowering us, Daddy had the skunks scent glands removed and gave them rabies and distemper shots.

Stinky, the female, had one white stripe while Butterball, the male, had two white stripes. They were adorable pets. Nocturnal by nature they roamed all over the house and slept most of the day. They were fed worms and grubs, apples and what they liked best, scrambled eggs. When they were in a playful mood, they would run toward us, tamp their front feet (natural defensive method) and back up. Both skunks would curl up in our laps or lay on their backs to have their tummies rubbed. Because of the spray, most carnivorous predators leave the skunk alone. Only one natural enemy, the Great Horned Owl, can't smell the putrid casting of a skunk making it the winner of the food chain. We had the kits for several years and enjoyed their playful antics. It got to the point they needed a larger area to roam so Daddy gave them away. They went to a person in the country who had a large dirt floor pen with a screen top and fenced area. I was sad to see them go but it was for the best.

Next were two crows and one of them talked … you read right … I said talked. Contrary to popular belief, a crow's tongue does not have to be split in order for it to talk. Jim, the talker, was an ornery cuss and lived in a 20 x 20 chicken wired pen. Like all the other critters, Mother found him when he fledged from the nest. Every time I went inside his pen, he swooped down and jerked out several strands of my white hair. Jim liked anything shiny, especially my hair clasps or beaded necklaces. With finesse and a few claw gouges to the skin or scalp, he latched onto them and took them back to his nest. His nest was an old wood keg that Daddy suspended at the corner of the tin roof. Jim would perch on a wrist or shoulder and cackle in your ear. He could whistle, say foul ball, play ball and screech the words, no way. Sometimes he would scream making people who walked down the street turn to look and see if a child was being beaten. Daddy let him fly away as it was time. If you don't believe me about this crow that could talk, phone Verna Titsworth Bagley. She was our next door neighbor and can tell you all about Jim and his penchant for whistling at her.

It's hysterical. The other crow who didn't talk was Loudmouth. He had a crippled foot and wing and stayed in a pen on our front porch. Mother would let him out each morning and he drank coffee and tried to smoke her Kool shorts. This is fact not fiction.

What is apropos to this story is when Dan, the kids and I moved to our house on Mt. Vista. Skunks came out of the woods as fast as they could, stinking up the whole area. Stray dogs and cats found our house. My daughter, whose hair was golden blonde had a crow land on her head several times. He jerked out hair, cackled and then flew away. Was it Jim? I don't know.

After the kids grew up and moved away, the skunks are still here and a cat I love to hate won't go home. If you live on Mount Vista and love your grey cat please keep it at home. Because, it seems, all things come full circle as my story ends where it began. Mr. Talon, a great hawk, makes a routine visit to my back yard and loves cats. Enough already! I may be a hillbilly but I am not Ellie Mae Clampett.

"YOU'LL BE Sorrr-REEEEE!"

Do you remember these words, "You'll be sorrr-REEEEE!" Those words came about in the 1940's and turned into a familiar warning. These days it could reference almost anything, especially if you have a gut feeling not to do something wrong and do it anyway. It revolved from a radio quiz show, *Take It or Leave It*. It was a spinoff of the first show, *Professor Quiz* and its successor, *Uncle Jim's Question Bee*.

Take It or Leave It ran from April 21, 1940 – July 27, 1947 and had numerous hosts. The most familiar names I recognized were Garry Moore and Eddie Cantor whose years as host spanned from 1947- 1950. Jack Paar entered the picture as third host on June 11, 1950. As the show gained popularity on radio, its name changed to *$64 Dollar Question*. This series lasted until June 1, 1952. The show's premise, as you might guess, was to stump a contestant with questions he / she couldn't answer. If they answered the question correctly, they might opt to take a prize or continue with harder questions.

The first question, if answered correctly, was worth one dollar. Each successive question doubled the bounty by two. The seventh question was the final round. If a person was able to reach this stage of the game with correct answers, the loot was $64.00. The live audience would taunt the contestant with the words "You'll be sorrr-REEEEE!" if they chose to lay their winnings on the line to continue answering questions. I am quite sure a few contestants ate those words when they walked away empty handed.

As television grew to greater heights, a premier show entered the picture. People would be able to watch the faces of the contestants and scowl when an answer was incorrect. On June 7, 1955, the popular radio quiz show, turned television, changed to *The $64,000 Dollar Question*. Its sponsor was Revlon. The first contestant was Thelma Bennett who didn't make it through the first round but did win a 1955 Cadillac convertible as a consolation prize. Anyone making the cut to be on the show had different categories to choose as the basis of questions, such as jazz, boxing or Lincoln. Jazz and boxing I understand but what the heck is Lincoln ... president, automobile or penny? Again, stages for answering prizes started with one dollar and doubled. Depending on what stage you advanced secured you with more money. They could quit the game at any time or advance to harder questions. Should they reach the $8,000 mark, and answered with a wrong question, they lost the whole kit and caboodle.

The only person reaching the $64,000 stage was a marine, Richard McCutchen, whose chosen subject was cooking. He became an instant celebrity as well as Joyce Brothers and an eleven year old child, Robert Strom when they in turn answered all correct answers. Almost all winners became household names and went on to become renown in major endorsements. This show went on to become *$64,000 Challenge*.

Three years after the show took television audiences on a whirl wind, they fizzled. Not because they were not popular but two spin off games, *Dotto and Twenty-*

One, was so scandalous all the shows were yanked off television. Some of the shows deliberately bumped off contestants simply because they disliked them. They chose contestants by "market" appearance or which person would bring in more viewers. The questions fell in the same category. Supposedly, an IBM sorting machine to select cards for random questions was merely for show. It seems, every card was identical and those buttons pushed didn't connect to the IBM sorter.

Congressional investigations proved the shows were rigged as answers were given out before the show began. None of the people involved in rigging the shows were punished, other than having their hands slapped with suspended sentences. They did, however, find themselves in a cold locker from television producers not wanting to be subjected to their illegal ways. A few contestants sued to recoup losses but they never won a case.

The year 1959 saw the last of the big money give away quiz shows. In 1976 and 1999 resurrection was attempted for *The $64,000 Question* and *$128,000 Question* shows but it didn't come to total fruition. Instead, the British show, *Who Wants to Be a Millionaire*, was produced in American version. It had the same format as the forerunners, fifteen questions with money doubling until the final one million dollar answer. The only difference between the old and new format is the "life line" and other "throw me a hint" offered to the contestant. Game shows still exist and they will be around until some twit decides he / she needs more pocket change because the hole they burned in their pocket is growing.

SKIPPING DOWN MEMORY LANE

I have some $64,000 questions. Why, if they had such a good thing going did those persons not leave well enough alone? Were the dollar signs not large enough or were the ash trays in their limo overflowing? Was the little woman complaining about her pocket change being too small? Are they still hearing these words…you'll be sorrrREEEE!

http://en.wikipedia.org/wiki/The_$64,000_Question

AN ERA GONE DIM

Contrary to popular belief, Thomas Alva Edison didn't invent the light bulb. Fifty years before Edison, many entrepreneurial inventors had hands on arc and incandescent lighting.

In 1877, two years before Edison had a breakthrough with incandescent lighting; Charles Brush operated an arc lighting business. Arc lighting was used in street lights where an electric arc ignites by gas. A very high voltage strikes an igniter sending a current through the ballast and starter. It's a complicated process to which I won't elaborate. I am thankful I don't have any of the high powered, several thousand degree Celsius heat producing little monsters in my house. I do have many incandescent light bulbs. Knowing the bulbs will no longer be produced gives me pause to reflect.

Domestic manufacturing of incandescent bulbs by a major USA company has ceased. They pulled the plug, literally! They pulled it on Edison, JQ Public, and the good old USA by deciding their green could get larger by going to China. Geesh, Louise, when will people wake up and realize it is greedy green they want. Really, it was a mandate from our own government when President Bush signed the New Energy Independence and Security Act of 2007 (energy law) to go into effect 2014.

Apparently it was too costly to retrofit the incandescent bald bulb into a new compact fluorescent. They would move the plant to China to eliminate overhead costs (wages) and cash in on tax breaks in overseas manufacturing. Think of the lost jobs. There is a nasty little fly in the ointment and someone needs to use a fly swatter to eradicate its thousand global eyes. Perhaps, if the powers that be told those skyscraper owners in all the large metropolises to turn out unnecessary wattage usage, the energy law would be void.

Why does every light in large or small cities need to be turned on? It might be a gorgeous sight to view the great Christmas tree metropolises but good grief, it is light bulb dependence. Is everyone afraid of the dark, or what? It doesn't take a rocket scientist to figure out what an energy crisis is ... for cryin' out loud, turn out the lights!

A long time ago, in my youthful era, people were cognizant about saving and the term was not "green." It was called "resourcefulness" as we weren't wasteful with things we had. Somewhere and somehow, we all jumped the tracks, derailed common sense and became complacent. Our self-satisfaction caught up with us and we are desperately trying to save what we ruined. Green is good but even green has pitfalls. Everyone seems to want to go green; especially those who want to see your little "green backs" go flying out of your pocket. Green means getting close to earth and eliminating some carbon footprints.

How, pray tell, if I do away with the bald light bulb and go to one with a full perm will my carbon footprint decrease? Those little curly Q light bulbs are about the ugliest thing I have ever seen. They don't match anything in my household and would stick out like a sore thumb dangling from a drop light. If I only need it to be on for a few seconds, it takes those few seconds for the idiot bulb to light. It would be easier to use a flashlight. What if the size of the bulb doesn't fit your lamp? Rush right out, fire up the car engine, push noxious fumes into the atmosphere, get to the store and pay an arm and a leg for an adaptor. Oh well, it's just another hand full of greenbacks flying off to China. Another thing, if you have a lamp that uses three-way bulbs, you might have to toss the lamp into the trash if you poke one of those bulbs in its socket. Curly Q's are not dimmable. Uh oh, there goes another pile of greenbacks and the landfill will be overrun with scorched light fixtures. So much for the carbon footprint ... the pitfall is getting larger.

What will happen to the deco lights? Curly Q's can't flash so I guess those "Eat at Joe's" or all night casino lights will shut off unless they hire someone to constantly plug and unplug the signs. I can see it now ... help wanted ads begging for full time, night time, light pluggers ... provide references ... must be quick on the plug. With all that happening, a power surge is eminent and ka-pop, lights are dead ... gone to the instant death replay of voltage spikes. What to do? If one of these fluorescent light bulbs breaks, you run the risk of mercury poisoning. Hey, no, no, no ... tsk, tsk, tsk, you can't sweep it off the floor. You better pray it doesn't crash into the carpet because a hazmat team, charging fees out the kazoo, will be on you like ugly on ape. Where will they put the hazardous material after they swathe your house in a cocoon of plastic wrap? You best check your home owner's insurance.

What would you like to bet that any damage to your house by those mercury laden, over permed curly Q's is not covered? Shut your eyes and fling it into the trash can. There goes the landfill, real damage is done to our supposedly clean environment and another carbon footprint has grown to disproportionate size. It's a slow growing blob designed to send our money to China while we blink through dimming rays of light all because some twit didn't have enough sense to turn off an incandescent light bulb to cut energy use. Not to worry though, old baldy (incandescent) is not completely forgotten as the act does not include some specific bulbs nor does it include the existing use of stock bulbs.

Personally, I am on the bandwagon to save energy but I prefer bald light bulbs to permed cork screws. I think (my opinion only!) it's a bunch of horsefeathers that, we, the people, have to go into hock to appease some idiot in Washington who likes to see his / her name plastered on any bill / rider that will adversely affect all US citizens. Overzealous congressmen should burn the midnight oil (no light bulbs) and do their homework to save any kind of lost jobs and impose hefty taxes on those corporate giants who move "our" jobs overseas. Then, they have been in the dark for so long … they don't realize their light bulbs burned out long ago.

Go here to read what is not included.
http://energystar.custhelp.com/cgi-bin/energystar.cfg/php/enduser/std_adp.php?p_faqid=4913

ARTHUR STOP!

It's funny what a person hears on a sweltering summer's day. Funnier yet, is how two words spelled differently but pronounced almost the same can have a lasting effect on the brain.

Several years ago the temperature was much like it is today. Hot enough to fry eggs on concrete and melt asphalt onto the soles of shoes. I had no desire to go grocery shopping. In fact, consuming any type of food didn't appeal to me as it was too hot to eat. However, my Thursday weekly routine stared me in the face and I had no choice, we needed staples. Going early to the store, I thought, would get me back home before the heat baked my brain but it never happened. I like to talk to my friends who shop on Thursday and catch up on what we last chatted about … our lives turned soap opera. We always leave a cliff hanger when we go our separate ways and hope to pick up where we left off. It was a typical Thursday or so I thought.

Making sure I had everything in my cart, I proceeded to the check out. Over the chatter, bang of carts and an occasional intercom spout, I thought I heard someone yell "Arthur." As I looked around the perimeter, it appeared normal. I casually went through the automatic doors leaving the frigid air-conditioned atmosphere into a beastly, eyeglass fogging sauna. I couldn't see squat and was almost afraid to step into the yellow striped, hazardous walkway. As I peered over my fog laden glasses, I took a chance and hoped I wouldn't be squashed by an Indy 500, Suburban driven; I have a phone surgically implanted in my ear maniac driver.

I didn't get plowed over but all those horrid bubble gum spit outs that a body tries to avoid, was waiting for me. Unable to see where I was going because of white fog glasses, I stepped on a blob and smeared the sticky goop six feet from the front door. The more I tried to dislodge the pink, stringy mass the more it spread ... on me, the ground and wobbly cart wheels. The air was stifling while the humidity, along with the sticky bubblegum made my clothing adhere to the skin. It was like being caught in too tight size six when you need an Army tent. My toes stuck together inside my sneakers making my body feel as though I was walking on stubs. I didn't dare pull off the shoes as my feet, in desperate measure, would swell to disproportionate size. I needed a bucket of ice water ... gulped down or poured over my head.

It was a good thing I didn't try to coif my hair because I would have had to use a whole can of heavy duty instant freeze hair spray. I couldn't fathom putting a comb into a barbed wire hair-do. It would have been like a Venus fly trap, waiting to snap the comb under layers of cement spray. Humidity and cement spray is worse than salty sweat rolling into eyes. If those two combinations hit my eyes, rest assured, they would be plastered shut in a matter of seconds. Again, I thought I heard the word "Arthur." I wasn't hearing things as it was louder and more intense with the words, "Arthur, stop!"

Somehow, in the ghastly heat and bubble gum fight, I couldn't find my car. It was there when I went inside. I was vexed; every car seemed to be the color of mine.

What was happening to my Thursday? It or I was insane or damned near blind. The parking lot looked like a maroon color used car lot. Desperate to get out of there and go home before I had to eat sun fried bacon, I hit the horn and trunk button on my keychain. Pity sakes, my car was two isles over.

By now, I am sweating profusely and my glasses were barely hanging on my ears. I looked like something the cat wouldn't bury. Uh, oh ..."Arthur, I said stop!" went to a higher decibel and was closer to me. I knew any second poor old Arthur was going to be whacked in the head with a loaf of French bread, go sailing over the top of my head or be heading to the mortuary feet first. "Arthur, please stop. Stop, Arthur, stop!"

She was desperate and so was I. I wanted to get the hell out of Dodge and away from the two of them before there was a battle on the border. Finally, I reached my car, slung my purse in the passenger seat and locked the door. Now, it was time to un-cart grocery bags to the trunk. As I leaned over to unlatch the mesh cage inside my trunk, I heard heavy breathing ... right behind me. The macabre breathless word, "Arthur," sent cold chills up my spine. What was I to do? Crawl inside the trunk and slam the door or wait for them to go tooth and nail.

Before I could straighten upright, I heard a dull thud. I figured Arthur would join me inside the trunk, dead as a hammer. My throat went cotton ball dry wondering if an ax wielding crackpot was about to do me in. About now, I heard another tin sounding crash. Her cart and mine bashed into one another and I knew a fight was about to commence. I was eager to get my groceries in the trunk and turned around ... facing what I thought would be a 911 call.

My eyes got as big as saucers when I came face to face with a red faced, drippy haired, sweat laden woman with glasses hanging from the tip of her nose. At one point, she had to be neatly dressed but now, she was out of breath and panting ... just like me. I looked around to see if Arthur was standing there. He wasn't. I didn't see legs jutting from under my car or blood so figured she hadn't killed him.

Defuse the situation. "Nice day?" I said.

"Hell, no," she snapped. "It's too hot." She gasped for breath and reached inside her purse.

Now what? Is she going to shoot me? I hate this Thursday! Then, all of a sudden, she shoved copies of three books in my direction. "It's you; you're the author of these books. You know, I cried when I read this one, it's so moving. The other two made me laugh." She took a breath and continued. "I'm from Fort Smith but come here to shop for my mother. Someone told her you were here every Thursday but by the time I get here to shop, you're gone. I've been carrying these books around for weeks hoping to bump into you. I am so glad you stopped when you did because I can't take another step." She swiped her brow. "Gosh, I am so hot I can't breathe. Would you please sign them?"

When I told her what I thought I heard, we broke into belly laughter. As we sat on the edge of my opened trunk, I signed her books. "To: Kaye. You made this blistering, scary day from hell one I will never forget." Signed: Joyce, "Author ... I thought I was going to die on this miserable day ... Arthur!"

121

CHUG, CHUG, CHUG

Little Red Caboose, chug, chug, chug. Do you remember watching a train go by or counting the freight cars attached to the engine? What about the caboose? At one time, it was an integral part of the train as it housed conductors, flagmen, brakemen and other railroaders. Those men used the caboose as a home away from home when traveling from one state to the other. The conductors used the caboose as an office and it was there all the records were maintained. A caboose might have been at the end of the train but it was there to protect the train when it stopped. It was a vantage point for those men to check for hot boxes (a boxcar whose axel bearing wheels gets too hot and can start a fire), loads that might shift, or to see if any equipment was broken.

A flatcar was used in the early days with a makeshift cabin for shelter. In order for the caboose to be seen at night, red lights were attached to the rear. The red lights were called 'markers' meaning it was bringing up the rear of the train. Workers used coal or wood to fire up a cast iron stove for warmth or to cook a meal. Daddy told me the stoves didn't have legs and were bolted to the flatcar to keep them immobile as to not tip over and spill burning embers. As the years progressed, the lowly caboose, with kerosene lamps, came up a notch. It was still at the rear as that is what caboose means but with electrical generators becoming "state of the art" the caboose was modified.

SKIPPING DOWN MEMORY LANE

When you saw a caboose, do you remember the cupola at the top? In America, most of our trains had a small perch at the top with windows on all four sides. It was T.B. Watson, who in 1868, was told to turn over his caboose to a conductor of a construction train. Since he had no choice in relinquishing his small quarters he used a boxcar that had a hole about two feet square in its ceiling for a caboose. He put tool boxes and a lantern under the hole and sat with his head above the hole. It was he that suggested putting some type of box over the hole so he could keep watch over the train. As a freight conductor with the Chicago and Northwestern Railway, his ingenuity, in doing due diligence for the rail system, developed the cupola. Eastern railroads had a cupola in the center while the western rail preferred it at the rear.

Some railroad personnel didn't have a preference. ATSF (Atchison, Topeka and Santa Fe) wanted the caboose to face whichever direction they chose. It was their right to refuse assignment due to a rare union agreement clause that was used but it was not an everyday occurrence. However, not all cabooses had a cupola. Some had bay windows and extended or wide vision where it extended over the side of the caboose. Others were the Drover (livestock boxcar) and Transfer used in switching runs. The bay window was first used in 1923 with Akron, Canton and Youngstown but in 1930 an experimental model used by Baltimore and Ohio Railroad became favorable. These designs were used because old tunnels and overpasses didn't have a high clearance.

Not all cabooses were bright red. Some were yellow, dull green, silver, red and white or reddish brown. The little red caboose I came to love and watch as it faded in the distance started with the Santa Fe. In 1970, the Santa Fe was revamping a program in which its cabooses were painted bright red. The eight foot diameter Santa Fe cross herald logo was painted in bright yellow on both sides of the red caboose.

Do you remember the red and blue caboose light on the back of our red cabooses? In my collection of Daddy's old memorabilia, I have two of the vintage railroad caboose lantern lights, one antique Handlan St. Louis USA railroad caboose lamp kerosene burner, railroad tie tongs, oil and water cans and other items. You won't see these lanterns on any caboose and no longer will you see a caboose unless it's on a private railroad line, refurbished as a cafe or an excursion train like the Arkansas & Missouri that runs from Van Buren to Winslow.

Up until the 1980's we could wave to the conductor or watch the caboose amble down the tracks to its designation. It was a lonesome site as the whistle of the freight train echoed in the distance and wheels click-clacked down the track. A red light, attached to the caboose, was bright and then faded until it was a speck no longer discernable. The caboose was a signal. We knew it was safe to cross the tracks because of the little red caboose and its conductor. As progress took its toll on the train, computers and new age equipment replaced workers that took pride in making sure the train was in perfect order. Deemed dangerous for the workers because of slack run-ins or having them thrown from the train, the caboose became obsolete. Instead of the caboose and its flashing lights, FRED (flashing rear-end device) or EOTD, an acronym for 'end of train device' is placed on the last box or flatcar.

Its mechanism relays messages to the engineer through a computer.

Daddy, a Carman inspector, spent many a night and day in a caboose as he worked weeks at a time in Coffeyville, Kansas and Gurdon, Arkansas. Since the caboose was the only area he could ride between these places, the stories he told me about waving to little kids was heartwarming. I remember helping Daddy put apples and oranges into doubled up brown paper bags. Sometimes candy or nuts was added as a special treat. He put all the bags into a duffel bag and headed for the yards to leave Van Buren. He told me most of the kids lived close to the tracks in small run down houses. If it was early in the morning, bare foot pajama clad children would run to see the train and its little reddish brown caboose. It didn't matter ... sun, rain, the dead of winter's sleet or snow, children loved the caboose.

Two or three miles from towns, the engineer would blow the whistle. As the train slowed, Daddy said he knew the kids would be waiting for the train and then he would toss the bags of goodies to them. I asked him why he liked to do this thing and he told me their waves and wide grins made his heart smile.

The kids never knew who he was or why he did what he did. When I think of all the stories Daddy told me, I am reminded of a book, *The Polar Express* by Chris Van Allsburg, given to me at Christmas by my sister, Hazel. I often wondered if those children Daddy waved to thought the bell they heard (train's whistle,) the bags of goodies and its caboose was their path to the North Pole.

Alas, I will never know their dreams and aspiration but I do know and remember my love for Daddy's stories and the "*Little Red Caboose, chug, chug, chug.*"

ADDICTED TO CRUNCHY KERNELS

Ooh, I can still smell the tantalizing aroma. What I am about to say doesn't apply to me because I eat maybe three bowls a year but I don't know about your addiction to the crunchy kernels. I don't know if it's true but the industry, who should be in the know, says every person eats fifty-two quarts of popcorn every year. Do you realize, for every man, woman and child who consumes the munchies, it amounts to 16 billion quarts each year? Speaking of popcorn, it goes hand and hand with movie theaters or settling down in your home as you watch TV or read a good book.

Do you remember some of these theaters in Fort Smith? Believe it or not, some of them were before my time but others I remember well. The ones I remember are: Rex, Joie, Temple opened in 1927, Plaza, and Malco made up of Quartet, Twin and Trio, Minitek, the theater at Phoenix, and Carmike Cinemas. Those before my time were Fort, Hoyt's, Mystic, Sebastian, Uptown, Princess, Rialto, Palace, Victory and New Theater that opened in 1911. So many of these theaters were either closed or demolished. One that is in restoration is the New Theater, aka Malco, at 9 North 10th Street. In Van Buren our only theater was The Bob Burns Theater.

There were drive-in theaters and they were the 22 Drive-in on Highway 22, 71 Drive-in and The Skyvue on Midland. As I drive by the great Skyvue parking area, I can't help but have nostalgic thoughts. Surplus veins of memories flash by as though it was yesterday and in a sense, it is. In the fifties and sixties, going to a movie was exciting. It didn't cost much to walk through the doors to sit in luxurious seats or park your vehicle in the dead of night to swat mosquitoes while you watched one of the flicks. The Skyvue had a one dollar, car load night. Kids would cram inside the car, much like those telephone booth (world record 25) or Volkswagen (15 in 1971) overloads. Many cars had kids stuffed inside the trunk. You could tell which cars tried to sneak in too many people as the rear of the car dragged the ground. It's a wonder they didn't succumb to carbon monoxide poisoning. Somehow, the proprietors got wind of the sneakiness and started checking trunks.

The drive-in parking area was designed for the front end of the car to be parked on an upward slope. On the driver's side, a gray metal device with wire encased in metal, was attached to something resembling a parking meter. It was the sound system. You could hang it on the rolled down window or leave it attached to the meter. Up and down volume was your only choice. It really didn't matter as everyone had the volume up so high, it blasted sound for miles.

Most times, if you wanted to go to the concession stand you either went through the passenger side or took a chance in denting the driver's door from the sound system. The concession stand was in front of all the cars. From there the picture was projected to the screen and you weren't allowed to venture beyond the stand. Lines of hungry kids, teens and adults plowed their way and sometimes fought if there was a line struggle. Popcorn, candy and drinks and sometimes hotdogs were the favorites. Trying to handle and carry several drinks and boxes of popcorn back to the car was almost impossible, not to mention dangerous if you got misdirected or too close to a fogged up windowed car. If you weren't careful, you might try to get in someone else's car since most cars looked alike. It was a blast and one of the most popular places to be on a weekend.

In 1941 Van Buren used to have a theater called the Royal. I'm not 100 percent sure but in doing research, I found these two sites. Like everything on the web, you can't be 100 percent certain of accuracy. The sites (see footnote) indicate the name may have been changed to Rio in 1943. Both of these theaters were at 616 Main Street and sat 500 people. It was before my time.

The popular one I grew up to love was The Bob Burns Theater with 631 seats. I didn't count the seats but it's possible as the seats were so close together you could hear the heartbeat of the person sitting next to you. Droves of kids packed the theater on Saturday and Sunday afternoons. Sometimes a ruckus erupted from a surge of testosterones and an usher would shine a flashlight on those unruly kids. If the fight continued, they were ejected from the theater.

The best place to sit was on or near the back row as the view was not obstructed by bobble head kids. I liked it best as it was easy access to the concession stand and quicker on the draw. People at the back could tell immediately when the popcorn was fresh popped and then it was a mad rush to get the tasty, buttered, large ten cent bag morsels. Alas, they are memories as both theaters are no longer with us but popcorn has not fallen from favor. I don't want to forget those fun times we had because they were special but for some people, the past is the past ... no frills, laughter or excitement to recall. It makes me wonder why anyone would want to forget a part of their life ... especially a drive-in or building theater.

I think I will close my eyes and reflect on some more good times. Uh oh, now that I think about it, I better pop some corn. Otherwise, I won't be able to live up to the 52 quarts of popcorn since it is November and I have a lot of chewing to do before my year of consumption runs out. Somebody better provide me a wheelbarrow for my overloaded body and hand me a bottle of Pepto ... I am going to be sick as a junk yard dog!

http://www.cinematour.com/theatres/us/AR/3.html

http://cinematreasures.org/location/country=181&state=4&view=expand&show=all and

http://cinematreasures.org/theater/8771/

GO CARTS
Ingenuity pushed to the limit

They weren't fancy but they scooted. We didn't have cobblestone roads to make steering easy. Instead we had bumpy dirt roads and usually wound up in one of the deep ditches. If we were lucky, we managed to keep all our teeth intact and no facial lacerations requiring a trek to the doctor for stitches. We did bang elbows, scrape knees and rip clothing. Since our clothes were already patched from knees to backside, another wild plaid shirt or red checkered tablecloth cut into strips and sewn into patched on patches wouldn't make any difference.

We knew they wouldn't last through the day or draw attention to our clumsiness nor afford us any protection from what was to come our way. We didn't have helmets, knee or elbow protectors or steel toed shoes. What we had was hand-me-down clothes and shoes, sometimes too big or small, from older brothers or sisters. We made do with what we had in the way of clothing and enjoyed ripping to shreds what we couldn't stand to wear. It was the same with toys. If they were broken, we coped and refurbished them into a different form. Our ingenuity pushed the limits.

What made us climb into the wood crate? Insanity! Actually, all of us kids didn't think of danger and it wasn't insane. It was a form of fun and lasted until the last nail fell from the frame or a wheel dislodged or warped from a good whack from a huge rock. I'm talking about homemade go carts ... the kind of go cart kids threw together with stuff found in the dump.

At the time, old wood milk crates served a purpose far from housing milk. Those crates were made for kids eager to fly down a hill so they could land upside down on their heads. Sometimes two crates were put together for sturdier support and allowed us some leg protection. The frame of the go cart consisted of two planks nailed down on a single plank. It was what we called an "I" frame. At the back of the "I" frame, we attached the milk crate. The back of the crate supported our spine, maybe, while the front of the crate was cut out so our feet could get the go cart to move forward. The wheels were from old baby push carts we found at the dump. Since they were already on an axle, all we had to do was attach them to each of the 'I' on the cart. Most times they were wired on and we hoped and prayed they lasted until we hit the bottom of Henry Street. Our only steering mechanism was a long rope attached to the front of the axle. It was supposed to move the wheels in the direction we wanted to go but until we figured out how to do it, we only went in one direction ... straight.

As we became more secure with our makeshift go cart, we added old pillows for added comfort. We hoped it would prevent our backsides from bruising but it didn't. All it did was wad up under our rear ends making us lopsided inside the milk crate. I'm not sure which one of us came up with the next stunt ... the top of Cedar Street and Log Town Hill. The old road was treacherous and most times one-way in whichever direction a car traveled. Down the road we sped, dodging boulders and trying to stay out of the small branch between Washington and Lafayette Streets. Tiring of cracking our knees and dodging cars, we went to Arkansas Street. It was downhill all the way but still we couldn't get momentum because of cars.

As you might guess, some goober thought we should attempt going down Log Town Hill. Why we thought we could lug a stupid go cart up the hill only to turn around and go back down it, was more than stupid ... it was plain ignorant. Ooga-ooga, toot-toot and other sounds of beeping horns blared and a few choice words were yelled out the car windows. We waved and smiled as if we had good sense and hoped no one recognized us. Our venture didn't last too long. We were so out of breath that by the time it was my second turn to speed down the hill, the cart was nothing more than a lump of wood hanging onto battered wheels. It was fit to go back to the city dump or buried in a cistern.

Somebody snitched. When Daddy found out his little girl was trying to outrun an automobile on Log Town Hill, I was doing more than a two-step trying to convince him he would have done it, too. Daddy never spanked me for doing this wild haired stunt as he never had to do more than clap his large meat-hook hands together to get my attention.

My reasoning was that I was following him in his footsteps trying to do all the wild things he told me he did when he was a boy. He turned white as a sheet as I'm sure he thought the next thing I would do is blow up an outhouse or set off dynamite caps. I could see his belly churn trying to suppress laughter but, at the same time, I could see his face showed grief. He tried to impress the fact I was a girl and girls act like a lady. It was about this time in my life when I decided to put away the tomboy act and stay off the go carts. Besides, I hated it when my elbows were stubbed so badly, I couldn't bend my arms and my knees looked as if I had permanent scabby scars.

It was a fun time and I wouldn't change a thing. Well, that's not true as I would have changed four things. I would have worn a mask so no one could recognize me, been the first person going down Log Town Hill and I would have stayed at the bottom and watched them drag the stupid go cart back up the hill.

THE LOVE IN GRANDMA'S HANDS

Hold up your hand if you still have a homemade quilt in your house. Did your grandmother or mother make it or did you buy it at a flea market or specialty shop? Have you quilted or watched as nimble fingers guided the needle in a rocking stitch to secure tiny loops of thread through the fabric? Have you collected old pieces of scrap material and shoved them in a corner of the closet so you could try your hand at making the warm coverlet? There are all kinds of quilts. Some people make quilts by the old fashioned long arm style or sewing machine. Making a quilt is not as easy as one might think and it takes longer than a week to throw one together…it takes months.

The earliest type of quilt (quilted linen carpet) was known to be from Asia in the first century C.E. It was found in a Siberian cave tomb. The pictures on the quilt were of animals with a spiraled border. Ancient Egyptian quilts depict humans wearing quilt clothing. Even though quilting has been a huge part of European needlework as far back as the fifth century, C.E., it's thought the Egyptian cottons were part of the trade in the Mediterranean taking goods to Europe. Those persons learning how to quilt in Europe had a major impact on Colonial times as they brought the needlework to new land across the water.

Later, in the 1800's most women didn't use the block pattern but made quilts from whole cloth fabric.

SKIPPING DOWN MEMORY LANE

It wasn't until the Pioneer days that women used a paper pattern to fashion block quilts. As a pattern, they used almost any type of paper to sew the blocks together. Some old quilts were found with old letters, catalog pages and newspaper clippings still stitched inside the handmade beauties. It's thought the paper added insulation to the interior of the quilt. Well, we've come a long way since then and modern day fabrics and batting and sewing machines take the guesswork out of quilt making. It's too easy.

One thing I know was not easy was Grandma's way of quilting. Grandma Hawkins had a quilt frame. I remember months on end how the frame took up one bedroom with no space to walk. It was Grandma's solace, a place to go when she was fed up with the world and its objectives. She found it a release, of sorts, letting ragged nerves release and calm with a needle and thread. It was also history in the making as what she was taught in her youth, made its way to me. I will never forget asking her why she needed so much stuff to make one quilt for a double bed. I had a lot to learn as I watched how and what she did.

She was meticulous in the routine. She started with a pattern, maybe a simple 4 x 4 block or wedding ring circles made from paper. Cut out blocks of various colored materials was piled in brown paper bags and labeled. Material needed to match or compliment the surrounding squares and all had to be exactly the same size. If a square seemed out of place, tacking thread soon found its way to the trash can. It was back to digging through sacks of colored squares ... all for a perfect shade and shape of material.

Tacking squares of material together with perfect straight angle corners took patience. Each successive block was ironed flat. The ironing board and iron stayed stationary in the bedroom ... another item to maneuver around but it was a necessity. We measured and measured and ironed and ironed. The completed top had to be a certain length and width to join its batting and back cover. Tons of batting covered a small corner of the bedroom. If you accidently hit the mound, it created a landslide toward other piles of ... "I put it where I want it. Don't move that stuff or you will be in trouble"... material. It took forever to do a quilt top and I felt I would turn her age before I turned into a teenager. I wouldn't say I was bored but danged near it.

I became eager to sew the quilt on the frame to find out why Grandma had a love for this odd shaped friend. It was a weird contraption made out of four pieces of wood with butterfly wing nuts and bolts. On the long ends of wood, a sturdy fabric was stretched taut while the short (width) ends were basted to the cloth. As the quilt began taking shape, the wing nuts were loosened, removed and placed into another position. Then, the quilt was rolled under to proceed to the next block of material. Although my stitches were not fine like Grandma's or Mother's, I soon learned the necessity of using a thimble. After I pricked my finger several times plunging the needle through cotton material and batting, Grandma rectified the situation by stuffing a wad of cotton into the thimble and taping it to my finger with a Band Aid. Somehow, a single needle found its way to every finger on my right and left hand and I was letting blood like a stuck hog. Several times, Mother had to tape thimbles to every finger on my right hand. It looked like I was ready to play a tune with castanets without the wrist strap.

SKIPPING DOWN MEMORY LANE

With each progression in making the quilt and adding the bright colored border to the edges, I knew the secret of the quilt frame. Those four pieces of long wood taking up space in a spare bedroom were there for a purpose. However, if you looked at them not knowing what they were, the splintery pieces of wood, on their own, could be used for many things. As the wood unfolded and tenderly caressed a masterpiece quilt top, it became a canvas … a canvas of Grandma's life, reflecting how she was raised and what she learned.

My quilt is very old, the one I helped sew. It's worn and tattered but love is still in the quilt. After years of wrapping sick children in its warmth, using it as a picnic blanket and draping it over chairs to make tents for small tots to play, it gave up part of its ghost. For some reason I can't seem to toss away the remainder of the ragged old quilt as it seems to have a life of its own. It may be an inanimate object but when I look at it, what I see is an old makeshift quilt frame and the love in Grandma's hands.

HALLOWEEN HAUNTED HOUSE

What do you remember about your childhood? Have you written anything down so your children can have a laugh or two? Do you think they would admit you were a kid and realize you were not 'old' when you were born? Somehow, kids think their parents were hatched or came from an alien planet and because of it, never lived one day having fun. When they are small they don't remember parents decorating for holidays so they will have fond remembrances. It's like they went to sleep and grew up being a teenager. It's universal until they have children of their own and then snap, a light bulb flickers overhead. They have an epiphany. What we did as parents suddenly becomes clear because they are now us and walking in our footsteps. Halleluiah!

When my children were old enough to don a costume and go trick or treating it conjured up my own experiences. It was a blast watching my children get wide eyed from an occasional "boo" or having them cower behind me in trepidation of shadowy figures. Even when they became older, Dan and I would find some way to liven the Halloween spirit. Ghostly figures, made of sheets dangling precariously from string, decorated the front porch. Sometimes bales of straw with pumpkins or corn stalks near the front entrance secreted a live body ready to jump out and scare the wits out of doorbell ringers.

SKIPPING DOWN MEMORY LANE

A particular Halloween gave new meaning in scaring the beejeebers out of too old to trick or treat teenagers. It was the dark ominous night of 1970. We rented a house from Lena Mae Smith, a niece of Roy Craig, and heir of an old two-story house on North 24th near the railroad tracks. At night, the house was spooky and even more on Halloween. The exterior was wood clapped with a long sloping front porch. The mansard roof made the house appear menacing. A neatly groomed privet hedge, in front of the house, bordered the oil and gravel street. The small sidewalk to our house could barely be seen. At the northeast grew a large walnut tree … a tree that would play an important role during Halloween.

The interior was beautiful for an old house and the staircase directly in front of the main door gave off eerie vibes. At the end of the hallway was an old pump organ. Pumping the pedals gave off a thumping, supernatural sound and it echoed down the narrow hallway. It sounded like someone wearing heavy shoes was encroaching on personal space. Using this organ, we recorded creepy music and placed the recorder in an upstairs window. It would be a magnet in drawing a crowd of curious kids.

Dan, the boys and I waited for darkness. It was time for goblins, ghouls and creepy nocturnal creatures to roam the streets. Dan, dressed in black, was a Werewolf. His face was painted white and his eyes were outlined in black. Fake blood smeared his lips and he wore artificial fangs while an old pixy wig cupped his face with hair. He and the boys set out for a night of absolute terror while I stayed at home with our four month old daughter, Lori. Even though I was home, I wasn't idle. My outfit included a long black wig teased to stand out in all directions, a black flowing negligee over black clothing and my face was white. The staircase was the perfect harrowing stage of fear. I turned on the tape recorded music that was in an upstairs window and waited.

Dan and the boys threw people into tailspins. His attire was out of the ordinary and with the boys dressed as small Werewolves, it added to the confusion. Little kids screamed in unison while their parents threatened Dan with bodily harm. The parent of one child (we knew them personally) requested Dan to meet her daughter on the front porch. Poor little thing came unhinged, did a tap dance, and left a puddle on the floor. Two men, waiting on their children to canvas the lighted neighborhood, were scared out of their wits. As Dan leaned inside the car he growled, "Mister, you got a light?" Both men gasped, said a few choice words, put the car in reverse and zipped backward down the street. It was one episode after the other and Dan was hysterical.

My role as Mrs. Werewolf was one to remember. The house was dark except for the porch. To add to the pandemonium, I replaced the white light with a red light. It cast shadows in weird hues but even so, I could see anyone approaching the house. The hallway was visible through the screen door and it added to the atmosphere. In very large bowls of water, flickering Tealight candles cast shadows and swirled them on the shiny hardwood floors and ceiling. I was sitting half way up the staircase waiting for the right moment. Several young children were apprehensive to venture too close to the front door but with a little persuasion, they happily accepted the pre-packaged bundles of candy. It got quiet…all for the eerie music. Then, a car stopped outside. It was full of teenage boys and I watched as they neared the front porch. It was foreboding all the way and their footsteps became slower in motion.

One boy said, "Go on up there. There is nothin' up there that'll hurt'cha."

Another replied, "From where I'm standin', I wouldn't be too sure!"

"Are you a coward?" one yelled out from the safety of the hedge.

About this time, the black walnut tree dropped several large walnuts directly on the front porch making a big thump. As if on cue, a neighbor's calico cat scampered across the porch and let out a big crawrrr. One kid let out a whoop and ran to the side of the house. The other boy dropped to his knees as if in prayer. The commotion awakened my daughter and she gave out a blood curdling scream. Her scream triggered a howl from our bulldog. As I descended from the stairs to comfort my baby girl, I held a flashlight under my chin and it made my body appear as if it was floating in space. A lighted railroad lantern swayed in my left hand. It was chaos.

"Lord, help mercy! What's that coming toward us?" a burly boy screamed.

"What ... what is that? Start the car! Somethin' is screamin' in there. It sounds like its bein' killed!" another boy hollered.

"This place is crazy and it's haunted! Somethin' bad is in there and I'm not goin' to find out what it is."

One kid plowed over the other and another tried in vain to go through the hedge. As the car started, the boy wedged inside the hedge told them to wait on him; they weren't leaving him to be eaten by whatever was roaming inside the house. Gravel flew through the air as those kids raced toward the next street.

Halloween 1970 was one to remember. I laughed so hard tears streamed down my face and when Dan and the boys came home, it was laugh central. The next day, I saw the same car full of boys drive slowly by the house. They were eyeballing what they thought was a haunted house. What did I do? I screamed, "BOO!"

Have a happy Halloween, everyone, but make it a fun and safe memorable event for your children. P.S.: Happy Birthday, Daddy!

IN THE WILD

In one of my stories I told you about the fondness I have for poke salad. Did you know there are other wild edible plants? One is a pesky little weed we all try to exterminate when our yards become green in the spring. It's the dandelion. This lowly plant can be used for a variety of things. Chop it up and use it in a salad, an herb, or you might find this strange, but as a coffee substitute. Early in the spring when the young shoots emerge from the ground is when to harvest the tender leaves. You must do this before the plant flowers. Some of you might find the taste a tad bitter but they contain a lot of Vitamin A. Cooking them several times will remove the pungent bitterness and it almost tastes like spinach. I haven't tried the trick Mother used. If Mother ran out of coffee, the roots were ground fine, dried for a few days and used as a substitute for the dark brown java she enjoyed. Tasting it once was enough for me because my lips puckered. Been there, done that and don't want to do it again.

Do you know what a water chinquapin is? If you have ever been near a large pond and a strange looking stalk with a hard, brown dried flower juts from the water, it's a chinquapin. Actually it isn't the flower but the seed pod. A chinquapin is a relative to the water lily. The foods from the chinquapin are numerous. In fact, the entire plant can be eaten. The broad green leaves are cooked in the manner as you would spinach and the seeds (inside the pod) can be roasted or boiled.

The tuber or root stock can be baked and tastes as sweet as a sweet potato. The American Indian used the lotus plants as a food staple. Best be careful when you extract one of the delicacies from a pond or you might have to fight off a water snake.

Lamb's quarters, sometimes called goosefeet because the leaves look like a goose foot, is delicious. Most yards have the plant growing wild but for the most part it's considered a nuisance weed. This edible plant tastes like chard or spinach with a distinct wild flavor. I would put it in the category of kale with sharp barbs and collards with tough stems but it's remarkably delicious. The young leaves can be used in salads. Giant Goosefoot (Magentas preen because it has a magenta hue to its growth) or lamb's quarters can be found at most seed retailers. All you have to do is steam the leaves to wilt and add your favorite seasoning.

Would you believe me if I told you wild cattails are edible? They are but don't mistake them with the poisonous calamus or daffodil. The only way you can be sure you have the right plant is to see the fluffy brown (looks like a burned corndog) seed head. The young shoots taste like a cucumber. These plants grow in marshy areas and bogs. It's best to harvest them when the ground is dry and before they flower. The brown seed heads (considered the flower) can be dried for use in ornamental flower arrangements but take heed, spray them with hair spray or shellac before you take them indoors. As the winter heat inside your house dries the seeds, it will explode into millions of fluffy, airborne particles. Take my word for it; they are harder than heck to clean up.

SKIPPING DOWN MEMORY LANE

The wild onion/garlic is tasty. Known as ramps, wild leek, ramson or spring onions, they taste like a combination of onion and garlic. These, too, are considered pests for the gardener but can be used in cooking. Mother preferred to use these instead of store bought because of the pungent taste. She used them in soup, stews, and cornbread and mixed them with scrambled eggs. Two of her favorite recipes called for regular onions. One is Chickasha Meat Balls made with ground beef and pork, eggs slightly beaten, dry bread crumbs, milk, nutmeg (not optional), salt, pepper and grated onion. I would help her gather several hands full of wild onions and then mince the entire scallions and bulbs. Sautéed in a dollop of butter, they were combined with the rest of the ingredients and then shaped into small balls. After they were fried, a portion of the milk was used to simmer the meat balls. The other favorite food was Otoe Bread. It didn't call for onions in the recipe but Mother added them anyway. It's fried bread made with flour, baking powder, salt and hot water. This simple Indian bread is lightly knead, shaped into ovals and deep fried. When cooked the Otoe swells up like a round hollow ball and Chickasha Meat Balls are inserted inside the bread.

There are so many wild foods free for the taking but make certain they are free of pesticides and know what you are picking. Clover, chickweed, burdock, prickly pear, rose hips, some viola (wild pansies), and the list continues. They grow wild in our yards, in fields and roadways. Before you go out and dig up what you think is edible, invest in a book of useful wild plants. My favorite book is *The Herb Society of America New Encyclopedia of Herbs and Their Uses*. It lists what is safe, how to grow them, poisonous or not, allergenic properties and has over fifteen hundred photographs. Even with this book I lean on major caution. My motto is "If in doubt, don't put it in your mouth."

We aren't in the pioneer era as our forefathers were and don't have to rely on wild plant sources to survive. Even so, some people still enjoy foraging for wild foods. Remember, you need to be able to identify each plant before someone has to identify you!

LITTLE THINGS MEAN A LOT

Kitty-cornered from where we lived on Henry Street was a neatly groomed yard with sweet smelling roses and flowers. Around the yard was a high concrete wall or so it seemed. The concrete fence, set back from the dirt road, soared high above my small stature. Hard as I tried, I couldn't jump high enough to peer over the fence.

A slope held small buttercup and larkspur flowers to keep erosion at bay. Sometimes wayward seeds would find a crack in the concrete fence and began growing. Their roots hinged tight in those small crevasses. It was elegant to see the pink and purple flowers droop from a dangling basket made from concrete. The entryway to the house had a metal gate and it was always shut. It was to keep their black dog, Blackie, from escaping.

Once inside the yard, a concrete walk led you to the front porch. The white painted porch was engaging with cushioned Adirondacks and a small table holding a vase of flowers and a Bible. Their back yard continued with roses, a vegetable garden and a detached garage. Most of the time, they walked or used public transportation but an old, light blue/green Chevrolet was driven when necessary.

The interior of the house was immaculate. As you walked in the front door, a staircase was immediately to the right. It took you to bedrooms on the second floor. A long hallway, with shiny hardwood floors let you to various downstairs rooms. On the south side of the hallway were two rooms. The front room contained beautiful antique furniture and grand pictures hanging by long tasseled ropes secured at the crown molding. Next to this room was a massive dining room. A mahogany table to set eight persons was set off with a white runner. Right in the center of the table was a vase of flowers as they came into season. During the winter, fronds of cedar or juniper berries cascaded from the vase. It was always beautiful. Directly to the west from these rooms was the bathroom. It always smelled of delicate perfume and talcum powder. Across the hall was a bedroom and sitting room. The kitchen was at the back of the house. Although I can see these rooms in vivid color, it is the aroma I continue to smell from these gorgeous pictures. I can close my eyes and smell collard greens with onions and bacon, potatoes and onions cooked in hog lard and fried corn fritters. The whole area was a magnificent picture as were the people living in the house.

It was not merely the sights and smells that enamored this child's mind but music. Tons of classical, jazz, boogie-woogie, and popular songs filled my heart so full; I exploded with song. It got to the point, I knew all the keys and when the "magical fingers" were going to modulate chords. Music danced over my head ... whole notes, half notes, quarter notes and major and minor chords. Quite often "Dorian minor" (D minor chord in the key of C major) could be heard all over the neighborhood. The minor chords to me were mysterious, dark and soulful and I found out they are used in jazz tunes.

Almost every day, I would sneak off and go sit on the neighbor's porch. The music was like a magnet pulling me toward the house. I would curl up in one of the Adirondack chairs and sing whether I knew the words or not. Usually, the lyrics were familiar but if not, I sang my own rendition. Most times, Willie would come outside and tell me if I was going to sing to his ivory keys, I might as well come inside. Oh the sight of the piano! It was a black lacquered baby grand Steinway sitting right in the middle of the front room. The antique sofa and arm chairs were placed precisely so each person could hear each note from the piano. Its top unfolded, raised to the ceiling by a single metal rod opened the sound. Beautiful music reverberated throughout the house and I was in sheer heaven. Many times I would fall asleep while listening to Willie play the piano and then, he would carry me home.

In desperation, Mother had to put cow bells on our gate to let her know when I was hell bent for leather to bolt across the street. There was another way to escape ... I climbed the fence and pitter patter ... across the street I went. Even though I knew how to sing, Willie taught me how to lean into notes, wail the blues and make the notes cry. He always told me never be afraid to belt out the words and if you mean it, feel it when you sing it. He used to play *Always* by Irving Berlin, Sammy Cahn's *Be My Love, In the Mood* and *Chattanooga Choo Choo* by Glenn Miller, *Boogie Woogie Bugle Boy* and *Beat Me Daddy-Eight to the Bar* by Raye-Prince and *Little Things Mean a Lot by* Kitty Kallen.

William "Willie" Wrice was the principal at the old Douglas School and from there went to Lincoln High School as the Director of Music and he also taught geography. He was known for forming the first 40 piece marching band at Lincoln High School in Fort

Smith, Arkansas. When he retired, he taught piano lessons in Van Buren. Willie was an accomplished piano player and teacher and had numerous students who learned under his masterful hand. He read music and could play tunes by ear. Mamie Wrice, the eldest, was born into slavery and lived in the music house with Willie. When Mamie became ill, their half-sister Mattie Scott West and her husband, Sam Lyons West moved from Charlotte, North Carolina to care for the ailing Mamie. Mattie also worked for Mrs. Caroline Scott and her daughter, Frances Scott, whose house overlooked the Arkansas River.

Frances West Malone, daughter to Mattie, was a maid for Jerome Ney of the Boston Store fame and came home various week-ends. When Willie and Mattie were no longer able to care for themselves, Frances quit her job and cared for them. J.T. West, a nephew to Mattie, was also a piano player and guitarist. Today, he is Jeffery Unit Director at the Fort Smith Boys and Girls Club.

At the time, I didn't see "people of color" and I would ask them how come they could tan in the sun and I couldn't. Mattie would say, "Child, your eyes are so blue they can't see color." She told me about the "n" word, what it meant, where it was derived and why the "n" words sometimes applies to other skin colors. What she told me was not derogatory to any race but what a six year old could comprehend. Her delicate words made a lasting impression. Even today, I hear her words. "It's not important what color skin covers the heart. The heart knows no color. It's the mind that makes the skin a dirty color and gives the heart its ache."

It was a sad time when each of them died but they left me with many fond memories. As I think of the songs I sang to Willie's remarkable talent, it's *Always* those little things that mean a lot.

MELT THEM DOWN!

This is Sunday 15. For several weeks while traveling to and from the hospital, the things I have encountered have been too much. Not the hospital but localized nuts. It took me back to the time my dad, the speed merchant (I mean four wheels), put metal to the pedal like the actual devil on manufactured speed.

It was 5 a.m. one morning as I was coming home from the hospital. It was pitch black outside except for stop and street lights and merchants that stay open twenty / four seven. At that time in the wee hours, it was amazing how many cars pounded the pavement. I watched as a few motorists obeyed the traffic laws but the majority of them must have had beans burning on a stove. They weaved in and out of lanes as though they were looming a blanket. The blanket had to be sixty miles long.

Right off Garrison Avenue in Fort Smith, Arkansas I had to stop for a red light. In front of me at the stop light, two men each of them in separate cars, revved engines. I knew what was about to happen. I wasn't wrong but extremely thankful I was behind their insanity. It was the same atmosphere in *American Graffiti* where teenagers were doing the Saturday night car crawl. The only thing different was that it was not midnight and Wolf Man Jack was not growling on an a.m. radio station or taking requests to send out to a special friend. I didn't see Richard Dryefus or the

Cadillac with the mysterious woman. There were no teenagers standing in front of the lunatics waving a flag to signal go or at the end to declare a winner. Neither car was a jalopy but newer models. They were low riders, maybe an inch from the ground, b-bopping with under supports doing an axel grind.

I watched as the hub caps whirled backwards while the cars were sitting still. It made me sick to my stomach thinking my car was moving forward. I kept pressing my brake to make certain I wasn't moving forward. It was making me bleary eyed from the up and down motion of the cars and hub caps doing a hula dance. As the light turned green, motors turned up an octave, tires barked and squealed while I watched two overloaded testosterone males shoot down the road. They were hell bent for leather to see which car was the best for dragging. The stop light, a block away, didn't have time to turn green and it would have been all time mayhem if another motorist pulled in front of them. I was sitting in a puff of smoke as rubber melted from the wheels. The first words from my mouth were idiots and where are the police?

One thing I'm not is a speed merchant. On occasion I do exceed the speed limit but only a couple of miles over the designated postings. I'm never impaired or lacking in the reflex department. After the episode with the drag strip idiots, I hoped nothing would happen again. Wrong! This day I was in a hurry but I should have stayed home a few minutes longer before leaving my house. As I waited for a car to pass my driveway, I backed out and proceeded forward. A slow as molasses female driver impeded my urgency to get to the hospital to be with Dan, my husband. How I wished I had an "ooga, ooga", freight or fog horn under the hood of my car. I kept telling her to get out of my way but her windows were rolled up. She didn't hear a word I was screaming but I did get a raspy voice.

I hoped she would turn off on a side street but nope, she was on a mission ... a slow terrapin moving mission. She lollygagged, stargazed, watched birds in the morning sun and dodged pebbles in the road. I started to honk my horn and go around her but knowing how she was driving might have made her veer in my direction. I opted against it as it was part of a residential area and illegal. At four miles per hour in a thirty mile zone, I sat back for the ride. I figured she would turn left at Arkansas Street. Nope, she went right. I was trying to stay a car's length behind her. Now we intersect with Knox Street. Oh goodie, she gave a left hand signal which meant I could do the speed limit. She must have turned it on by mistake because I dogged her tail till we got to Main Street. She went straight toward the interstate and I turned left at the courthouse. I could relax and get on to the hospital. Lo and behold, she sped up, turned right at the courthouse where the old jail used to be, paused at the stop sign and turned right ... right in front of me. I slammed my brakes and laid on the horn to avoid a collision. She smiled ... I said a few choice words.

Now we are at the bridge stoplight. Please let her go to Barling and away from me! Shoot fire, it didn't happen. This little old lady was going to Fort Smith but instead of going forward, she stopped at the yield sign. There were no cars within two blocks of us. While we waited and waited and waited, I could have eaten a three course meal. By now, the cars are coming at full force and she is still sitting there. I thought what is she waiting for, Christmas and Santa Claus to open presents?

It took; it seems like, fourteen minutes to go two miles. At last, I was able to go around her on the bridge. As I passed her, it was a wonder she was able to drive. Hunkered down in the seat and barely peering over the steering wheel, this little woman had to be ninety years old. I wondered if her feet were on the accelerator or if she was letting the car go on its own. Either she was using the steering column brake or her car realized she needed to be controlled. I must say, she had guts and stamina to venture onto a busy thoroughfare. Then I thought, there is a reason for me to slow down and I did. My impatience turned to calm and I got to the hospital when I needed to be there.

There is one thing I request. God willing I get to be ninety years old, somebody... please take my keys and bury them in the back yard. If you want to, melt them down and make a necklace, keychain or dog tags out of them but for goodness sake ... get me the hell out of my car and don't let me drive!

OCTOBER MORN

It was about this time of the year when I first noticed it. This particular week-end, my seven year old eyes took in all the magic the world provided in its quest of seasonal changes. The porch at my house on Henry Street faced the north and west. The vistas, directly to the north, were not all that memorable as the houses, in those directions, took up the majority of what I could see. To the west was a pecan tree that Mother planted when my sister was born. I loved to climb the tree but it took up too large an area for a porch swing. Facing north, our swing dangled from the edge of the porch. It was a deliberate move on Daddy's part because he knew I would swing too high and bang into the side of the house. Daddy hoped the porch swing would be a deterrent in keeping me out of the tree and off the roof of the house ... another place I loved to sit as it was quiet. I could see beyond the world, or so I thought. He had me pegged.

It was a cool, crisp morning-the kind of morning when a hint of frost is on the horizon. I knew the frost was hanging somewhere but the rime hadn't made it to the blades of grass. Maybe the delicate dew drops, hinged inside the leaves of trees, were too tired to fall to the ground. Although the grass was tinged with moisture, it wasn't the white crystalline ice I liked to touch and pull between my fingers.

SKIPPING DOWN MEMORY LANE

The scent of sweet mown grass lingered from the day before, as Daddy, like most men, hoped it would be the last time the blades turned on the push mower. The scent of bacon danced in the air and the aroma of fresh brewed coffee floated seamlessly toward my senses. This October morn beckoned the aromas of hickory emanating from a campfire, pumpkin pie spices seeping from an oven, and fresh washed linen on a clothesline. It was poetry in motion, a balance of sight and senses in sync.

As I looked toward Poplar Street to the east, the steep dirt road with rocks jutting from the earth caught my attention. It was a road that came alive in shadows. Massive trees hovered in unison causing the rocks to appear as dancing shoes. The tree limbs, swaying to and fro from the slight breeze, made the rocks glisten as if someone was pulling marionette strings. It was at this moment, I saw the most magnificent sight.

The morning sun, trying its best to jump over the trees to greet the world, showed brilliant hues I would never forget. The vibrant green oak leaves on limbs towering toward the sky and sycamore and elm leaves whispered shades of gray. A transparent mist hovered over the trees and the once exciting green colors became void. It was as though I was looking at a black and white picture trying to develop without success. The tips of leaves were outlined with brown not quite eager to turn ocher or dull red. They were in transition, a seasonal change to mark another year's growth.

This time I was not sitting in a porch swing but it was early in the morning. I was in my front yard eager to work my flowerbeds before the sun had a chance to shoo me back inside my house. The same sensation crept upon me, one that captured me as a seven year old. It was déjà vu. The grass was wet with morning dew but yet, the frost had not crept into the picture. The air was crisp and curled around me making goose bumps bristle my flesh. The cup of coffee I placed near me drew me into its fragrant aroma. Hickory smoke, from Dan's BBQ smoker, flit the air teasing my taste buds.

As I looked toward the east, the sun's rays bounced through neighboring trees and flashed my memory. Various shades of gray did a ballet through the majestic sunlight. This time, the tree trunks and limbs were dark brown against the backdrop of misty tones of gray and I stood there in awe. It was a captivating moment and it made me realize the month of October holds a particular roll of enchantment on nature's beauty. October is the autumnal season where things hang in limbo until twilight sprinkles its confetti of gold, rust, yellows and reds. It tickles the fancy to cozy under a warm blanket and sip apple cider. It's the end of harvest; a time to lay things by for the winter and to enjoy beauty made only by the will of nature.

Twice in my life, dawn approached and nudged me to take sight of my surroundings to look at a perfect picture. As I stood there, fixated on the beauty of a sunrise and the delicate balance of nature, I put down my shovel and watched the sun erase the misty watercolor canvas. It was gone in the blink of an eye. It was the alpha of things to come. Beautiful but eerie it reminded me of Hans Christian Andersen's story of *The Ugly Duckling*. Now, I am anxious to watch the next round of hues as the trees and sun create the fall extravaganza in a giant paintbrush burst of colors. It will be nature's omega, a beautiful swan.

OLD FORECASTING

Several weeks ago, Dan and I began tearing out an old border to one of my flowerbeds. In the process of unearthing rotting landscape, hundreds of black and red wooly worms began scooting across the ground. There were literally hundreds of them hiding under soil, leaves and inside the dirt. It reminded me of what Grandma Hawkins used to say. "If a wooly worm's hair is thick, black, red or gray and they clump around in a ball ... be prepared to pile in the wood because the snow will be heavy when it falls." Good grief, if this saying holds true then the snow this winter will be three feet deep.

It reminded me of other old time sayings that many farmers continue to use on a daily basis. They are not wacky rules but true observances. Red at night sailors take delight, red in morning, sailors take warning. Red sunrises have an ominous meaning. It sometimes indicates stormy weather. It can predict how animals and insects react. Have you ever watched ants and how they respond when the weather turns stormy and heavy rain is forecast? If the sky is crystal clear, ants will be crawling close to or on the ground. If you have a brick house, in fair weather they usually stay at least a brick or two from the ground. When the sky becomes overcast and rain begins to fall, the trails of ants' moves slowly upward, until they are out of torrential downpours. They have a natural instinct in knowing when to seek higher ground.

JOYCE RAPIER

Watching a squirrel scurry around my back yard as it picks up every acorn, says a lot. Watching it decimate the sunflower seeds in my bird feeder is as though it's telling me it needs to hoard as much food as possible. Poor little things don't realize my bird feeder stays full year round. Squirrels, in a gentle rain shower, use their tails like an umbrella as they flatten their tail over their heads for protection.

Field mice will chew through wood in order to get inside your house to stay warm. They know, in an uncanny way, food will be plentiful. Birds are another source for weather predictions. When the hummingbirds leave for Mexico, it signals me to watch for tiny, gray and white snow birds. Some birds flock together and line up on the overhead wires to stay warm. They take turns moving from one end to the other in order to keep the other birds warm.

Does your pet go berserk several hours before a storm? Have you noticed how the ears pin backwards and a sense of panic sets in on their calm attitude? It seems all creatures, large and small, have an innate ability to know more than humans for natural survival. If it was not true, there would be no animals in the forest. For many years, farmers have watched their farm animals and crops to know what the weather is going to do. Fur grows thick in the winter and animals huddle together long before the temperature drops.

If you look up at the sky at night and see a ring around the moon or the stars appear to have haze surrounding them, it means rain will soon fall. More often than not, it holds true. On a winter's day, if you burn wood in your fireplace, do you notice its directional flow? When the smoke exits the chimney, does the smoke go straight up or does it curl down toward the ground? If it curls toward the ground it means unfavorable weather.

What about fogs in August? I have heard if August has fogs, each of those fogs indicate the amount of snowy days we will see in winter. If it does happen to snow, a rule of thumb is, if snow lingers on the ground for three days in a row, it will snow again in one week. What about the persimmon seed? How many of you have cut open a seed to find the fork, spoon and knife? It's a strange phenomenon of nature that a persimmon seed can hold predictions of weather but it does. If you find a thick white spoon, many argue it means a wet, heavy snow is on the horizon.

Now, I don't know if any of these things are gospel in predicting weather forecasts, but keen observances of different things makes me wonder. I do believe, though, the old time farmers and farmers of today know all the signs of unpredictable weather patterns. It would be hard to live without Doppler forecasts and pinpointing areas of danger and siren alerts. I'm sure all of you know hundreds of old timey forecast predictions and they would be priceless for new generations. Write them down now so other people in your family will learn about forecasts from critters, insects and birds. They may not be able to talk as humans but talk they do ... we need to listen and watch. Best be filling up my birdfeeder before they peck the window telling me to get the lead out so they can have a Thanksgiving feast, too!

Happy Thanksgiving to all of you. Have a great day.

PARADES

In Van Buren, parades were major events signaling rodeo, home coming, and Christmas. Raise your hand if you worked on one of the late 50's or early 60's floats for one of those parades. An abundance of floats represented all types of organizations and were used in most every parade. Secrecy surrounded every aspect of design as it was a competition to see whose float's theme won first prize.

There were more than these three places used to build floats, but these are the ones I remember most. Jack's Motor Company, a warehouse to the east of Van Buren Feed Store and Rhodes Chevrolet allowed floats to be erected within their premises. Jack's Motor Company has always been in the same location. Before it was razed, the Van Buren Feed Store was at the upper portion of Main Street. It was right across the street from what is now Sharon's Dog Grooming Parlor that used to be a gasoline station. Rhodes Chevrolet was across the street to the east of the Crawford County Courthouse.

In two of these buildings, very large areas (mechanic work stations) saw hoards of young people hovering over their projects. The feed store personnel moved fodder for critters to the side allowing usage of their premises. To keep prying eyes at bay, butcher paper or sheets of newspapers hung from every window.

SKIPPING DOWN MEMORY LANE

People who owned flatbed trailers graciously gave permission to the teenagers to fashion them into exquisite works of art. Rolls of chicken wire, stapled to the edge of the flatbed draped toward the ground. Within each hole of the chicken wire, teenagers shoved tons of toilet tissue, facial napkins and colorful crepe paper for a decorative purpose. Rules were each piece of paper could not be shoved more than a thumbs length into the wire. It was a uniform style making the float desirable. It seemed like there were millions of one inch holes and each hole held three or four napkins.

Bales of hay were used as platforms for those sitting on the floats. Most times, the person owning the flatbed used his farm diesel tractor to tow the float in the parade. After all the hard work, we prayed for clear skies.

Sirens blared indicating the parade was imminent. Police cars, sometimes two at a time, inched along the street as they lead the procession. Do you remember the throngs of people lining the streets of downtown Van Buren waiting to catch a glimpse of the police car's flashing lights? Kids went wild with enthusiasm. Since the streets were closed to traffic, it was a time to dart across the street without fear. It was as though the children defied a car to invade the space set aside for their spirited event. As the sirens screeched closer, hearts became anxious as parents scurried to retrieve rambunctious kids frolicking in the street. Every inch, along the main drag and all the way out east end toward 15th Street, kids and adults waited with eager eyes to view someone they loved.

Majorettes, leading the band for those parades, wore short green skirts with a matching green and white fitted bodice and white boots with tassels. Every band member wore Kelley green uniforms and hats with white plumes. They were magnificent, keeping in step as music filtered through the air.

The rodeo parade was first in the year as it signaled the Arkansas / Oklahoma rodeo. It was a prelude to watching dust fly in the arena. The rodeo parade had almost every horse and rider in Crawford County and those from surrounding areas. Appaloosas, Pinto and Shetland ponies were fitted with elaborate adornments on tails and manes. Covered wagons and Model T Fords carried people with period clothing.

The homecoming parade, second in line to delight onlookers, was a gala event because it was an indicator of the homecoming football game. Homecoming queen and maids, bedecked in lacy, strapless gowns sat regally on a portion of the trunk on a convertible. With their feet resting on the back seat, they enhanced the sleek elegant convertibles. The convertibles were fashion accessories to the lovely royal court. Cheerleaders, wearing Kelley green skirts, white v-neck sweaters with a pointer emblazoned on the front and bedecked with a Peter Pan green collar, cheered their way down the street. Everyone knew the cadence and cheered with them. The Shriners, sometimes dressed as clowns, rode on small motorized scooters and caught everyone's attention as their dare devil stunts of sharp figure eights, wheelies and standing on seats made people gasp.

The Christmas parade was last. Different types of floats with religious themes made people ooh and ah. *Frosty the Snowman* and other Christmas characters perched or danced upon floats. Manger scenes sometimes included live sheep and other animals but it was the little children dressed as angels who stole the show.

The pièce de résistance was the caboose. It was a beautiful old fire engine. It was as though the engine screamed *Mighty Mouse's* slogan, "Here I come to save the day." During the Christmas parade, Santa Claus, in his bright red suit, sat atop the fire engine. Giant bags of candy surrounded him. As he dipped his hands inside the bags to toss the candy toward children, little hands waved in the air hoping to catch the sweet gifts from Santa.

Parades, by nature, are the epitome of down home country goodness. They are right up there with apple pie and ice cream because they bring the community together. It means something to everyone whether they are ninety years young at heart or a tot sitting on the shoulders of a parent. Maybe it is pride in knowing things, be it hard times or good times, is that a parade can bring joy to the heart and a tear to the eye. I think of our parades as an embossed greeting card because the participants care enough to give their very best. Harold Arlen said it all when he wrote the lyrics ... *I Love a Parade*, the tramping of the feet ...

FRUIT FIGHTS

Over the Thanksgiving holidays, Dan and I went to Colorado. We were going to visit our daughter, Lori, her son, Will, daughter, Naomi and husband, Dax and to see our new grandson, Dagon Blaise, who was born November 10. On our way through Oklahoma toward the plains of Kansas, I wanted to stop and pick an Osage orange.

Osage oranges got their name from Osage Indians as they lived near and in the range of the trees. Most of you know the fruit by hedge apple, hedge, bodark or horse apple. However, due to the amount of traffic and having to plow through barbed wire fences and taking a chance of spearing myself with stubby thorns on the trees, I gave up the notion. Besides, the cockeyed things were on the tops of trees and I was not about to shinny up a tree with the wind blowing ninety to nothing. I decided my best interest was to enjoy the view as we zipped past them. Seeing all these gorgeous Osage oranges brought back delightful memories of Chinaberries and persimmons.

In my yard were a Chinaberry and Persimmon tree and those two fruited trees allowed for some major splats. In the spring, the Chinaberry sprang forth with very fragrant clusters of lavender and white flowers. They grouped together like grapes hanging from stems. Then came berries, hundreds of cream colored fleshy berries but they were poisonous. We knew not to eat them because Daddy said they were kin to a pesticide and would kill humans and livestock. It didn't seem to hurt the birds because they scattered the seeds all over the yard. Well, maybe it wasn't the birds but well intended kids with pea shooters.

The five and dime stores had scads of pea shooters with tiny little ammo sealed in plastic bags. We wanted the pea shooter but not the dried legumes as they were too small to hold in the hand. The peas fell through our hands as fast as we tried to load our shooter and they were worthless. Enter Chinaberries! As the berries dried on the tree, the center (seed) of the berry became as hard as a rock. They were the perfect size to pack into the pea shooter and raise a pump knot the size of a goose egg. Mother was terrified we would shoot out someone's eye so she made us wear sunglasses. Actually, they weren't sunglasses but make shift glasses constructed from cardboard with a peep hole to see through. It was a pain in the keester to wear those stupid things because half the time we missed our targets.

The persimmon tree was another example of how the fruit came into play for us kids. In the late fall, our tree was loaded with bright orange fruit. They were edible but I hated the mushy things. They were orange and only good for hissing, long, skinny tailed, playing dead possums. When completely ripe, some of them were larger than a silver dollar. They were the best ones to use for the great persimmon fight. Needed was a limber, sharp pointed stick to skewer the persimmon on the tip. Sailing those things through the air resembled a scud missile. You never knew where it would land. I didn't like getting whacked in the head because it made the hair goop up with slime. If you slid on a bunch of the overripe persimmons, seeds and peelings stuck to the soles of shoes somewhat like that of a cow patty. You could do the splits before you could snap the fingers.

The Titsworths, my next door neighbors, had a very large Osage orange "horse apple" tree in their back yard. I don't know why we called them horse apples because horses couldn't eat the things and if they did, it would clog up their innards. As they are edible, squirrels love them. They open them with finesse, dig out the pulp covered seeds and gorge on them. Cutting into the skin of a horse apple is worse than trying to crack a pecan shell with the teeth … we did that, too! Opening the outer bumpy skin, a sticky milky substance adhered to the skin like glue. It was disgusting because the more you tried to rub it off, the more it stayed. It was the consistency of pine sap. The only saving grace was the orangey scent wafting in the air. It was delightful. The tree was beautiful and had character. Gnarly limbs reached upward and then drooped toward the ground, heavy with fruit. It was large enough for a tree house. Its trunk held five, nailed 2 x 4 stepping rungs and a wide platform perch. A sign, dangling from a limb, stated no girls allowed. The boys were always up in the tree plotting out a day's activity whether it was making homemade brew with wild muscadine or being flat out nasty. We knew what they were scheming as they were as transparent as Scotch tape. It meant the horse apples would find their way to unsuspecting females. The boys would hide inside the cistern, under the house, behind the outhouse or lay on the roof with a sack full of hatchet whacked horse apples. Horse apple segments, like persimmons, were shoved on the end of a sharpened stick and slung through the air making the war between girl and boy turn futuristic. I wished for a Flash Gordon ray gun to zap them unconscious.

How lovely it was to see all the Osage orange trees along the interstate. When I closed my eyes, the back yard tree, now gone, was standing there in all its glory waiting to embrace neighborhood kids and their escapades.

RED-EYE GRAVY

Some of you will know what I am talking about, others won't. You might snarl your nose to the prospect of eating red-eye gravy but I grew up eating the strange concoction. Do you know its origin? If not, this is supposedly how it got its name. Some call it a legend and fact but I don't know if it's true. You make the call. Back in Andrew Jackson's day (1767-1845) the well known general summoned his cook to tell him what to prepare for his meal. The cook was so hung over from drinking moonshine corn whiskey; the pupil's resembled glowing fire surrounded by whites of his eyes. As the general peered into the cook's eyes, he told him to bring some country ham with gravy the color of his eyes. Some of the general's men, overhearing what was said to the cook, dubbed the meal red-eye gravy.

Other names for this gravy include poor man's gravy, streaked, red ham gravy, bottom sop, or bird-eye gravy. It's made with bacon or ham and sometimes roast-beef depending on what area of the country you live. Different parts of the country mix in mustard or catsup making the color / taste of the gravy appeal to their taste buds. Biscuits, sometimes too dry with a single piece of ham, bacon or jowl sandwiched between, are usually dipped into the gravy to soften the insides. This is where the term "sop" comes into play as we sometimes sop our plates to get the very last morsel. To make the gravy you need blistering hot bacon or ham drippings. The only added ingredient is strong perked coffee. The reason the gravy looks like a red- eye is because the coffee sinks beneath the grease forming a round red iris. If flour is used to make a roué it merely makes white gravy, common gravy we all eat. It changes flavor and thickens when milk or other liquid is added.

When Mother was a small girl and lived in Frog Holler, times were hard and money was scarce. Flour wasn't something they ran to the store to buy. They either had it on hand or did without as stores were few and far between. The same thing applied to other staples and they got used to living a very simple life. They did without the things twenty-first century people demand on having at the fingertips. It was The Great Depression when Mother learned to cope and watch as grandma used the food they had in the cupboard. When they had money they bought staples in bulk and hoped the weevils wouldn't invade the precious commodity. Even if the little black bugs converged like the plague, nothing was discarded as grandma said the weevils were protein and edible. "Eating a few bugs won't kill you but you can danged well kill them by eating them. If you throw it out, you do without," was grandma's modus operandi. Coffee grounds were used more than once and no leftover brewed coffee was ever thrown to the hogs. She put the coffee in the ice box to use for red-eye gravy. Left over biscuits was made into bread pudding or chicken dressing. Grandma had to be doing something right by eating the little bugs and re-using coffee grounds as she lived to be ninety-eight years old.

JOYCE RAPIER

My first taste of red-eye gravy made a believer out of me and I learned well what Mother taught me. Mother told me if I ate it once I would eat it again. As usual, she was right on the mark. When I was small, I watched as she fried bacon in an iron skillet using a coffee pot as a weight against the shriveling pork. Putting the bacon aside, the drippings began to smoke. At that time, coffee was poured into the grease making it pop into the air and on the stove surface. It made a genuine mess ... a greasy mess and I was put off at what Mother wanted me to eat. It looked downright disgusting as when it settled the coffee sank beneath the grease making the red- eye. Then it was time to ladle it on to hot buttered biscuits. It took some coaxing to make me eat the stuff. Out of sight, out of mind! I closed my eyes, took a big bite and at that time I acquired a taste for General Jackson's red-eye gravy.

I suppose when it comes to eating red-eye gravy it is one person's taste against another's and how you perceive what is in front of you. Like grandma, telling us that eating weird bugs inside a bag of flour won't kill you, it's the same as eating red-eye gravy. It's not so bad when you close your eyes.

ROMANCE OF THE RAILS

When I was small, Daddy took me to the Van Buren Roundhouse (yards) and to the Missouri Pacific train station. While we were at the station and yard, he pointed out numbers on the locomotive passenger and freight trains. He told me that the train's number, going to and from Van Buren, indicated where they originated but was, for the most part, MP trains. Other freight and locomotives, in order to go back to the original starting point, used the roundhouse to turn around the massive engine.

The passenger locomotives were a strange lot and went from old coal burning steam engines in 1914 to deco in 1957. The coal car was directly behind the engine and a shovel was used to scoop up the coal to feed the fire. Dirty black smoke billowed from the top front of the engines as they chugged to get momentum and continued for the entire length of travel. Old wooden water tanks sat precariously close to the tracks and the trains took on water at each stop. A large water funnel, much like those used in a well, was connected at the top of the tank and the funnel could swing out over the train. A worker stood on the top of the train and guided the load of water to the train's tank car which was behind the engineer's station on the train. Without water engines couldn't run. At the front of the trains were pilots (cow catchers). It was designed to push or force anything on the rails to go upwards or

173

sideways to keep from derailing a train. Freight trains had cabooses but a passenger train only had a wire accordion gate at the rear of the last Pullman.

The Missouri Pacific train station was located between Drennen Street and Broadway right next to the railroad tracks. I loved going to the station to watch the trains stop and listen as the hot steam spewed from the wheels. Actually, it was not steam until the air was released from the brakes. Most times I would talk to the ticket taker whose station was on the east side of the building, watch the hands tick away time on the large white and black clock or climb an east side mulberry tree while Daddy conversed with all the men. Sometimes I would rummage through brochures housed in wall mounted slanted shelves and be in awe of pictures depicting faraway places. The brochures made me remember where we traveled on a passenger train. We went to Colorado by train and then took a touring car to the top of Pikes Peak and then to The Garden of the Gods. Inside the station, I would watch as people sat on the wood benches waiting on their exciting ride. I didn't ask them but wondered where they were going to visit. I wanted to tell them about going to Colorado and seeing the snow capped mountains. If it was their first train ride, it would be the most beautiful and mesmerizing ride of their lives. They would enjoy watching the train snake its way across bridges and through forested and prairie terrain.

The old Missouri Pacific station was beautiful with brownish red tiles on the roof and matching brick pavers surrounding the perimeter. The quad design was herringbone fashion and was laid about a couple of feet away from the railroad ties. It gave easy access to passengers to step down on a graveled area when the conductor helped them board the train. The stool, used for boarding passengers, had black metal legs with a rubber ridged platform. After passengers loaded, it was stored near the entrance of the train for its next use.

The conductor usually wore a black or blue wool uniform with white shirt and matching tie. His hat had a badge with the word 'Conductor' above the brim. The luggage carrier was nothing fancy. It had large metal wheels and a flat bed with wood rails on each end to keep luggage or packages from falling to the ground. On the south and north end of the station were white signs. The words Van Buren were printed in bold black letters. Ornate lamp posts, embedded in the earth, sat at the edge of the pavers. They were made of metal with the bottom portion in black and the rest in silver. At the top, a curlicue, somewhat like an ampersand, curled beneath an arch. The housing over the light bulb had the appearance of a Chinese worker's hat. The MP train station held a lot of memories for me but as passenger trains became obsolete, so did the station and it was demolished. The last steam engine for MP ceased in 1955 and passenger trains going north through Van Buren was March 28, 1960.

The Van Buren Roundhouse was another intriguing place. Not because of its beauty but the exactness of its construction. It was situated on the south side of the tracks close to where the access road to I-540 is today. A road to the structure was due south, then left, of the overpass on 4th Street by Allen Canning Plant as you go toward I-540. Twenty-one bays and matching rails for engines or boxcars which needed to be turned around were built and completed in 1943 by shop employees and the 748th RY (Railway) Operating

Battalion. My daddy, J.D. Brannam, was one of the employees. On occasion, I would go with him to the yards and watch as an engine or boxcar was driven to the center rotating device. The turntable would spin the engine to the proper bay, enter then back out on a different rail, rotate and return it to the direction it needed to go. It was a massive operation and took great skill in maneuvering the 120 – 240 ton locomotive. The tons depended on if it was yard, switcher or mainline engine. I was never allowed to get out of the car as it was a dangerous place to be, especially for me, whose inclination was to get up close to see how things worked.

At the time, locomotives only had one front operating direction. As locomotives began improving, an engineer was able to have front and rear positions where he could change the point of traveling direction in the cab. Alas, there was no need for the roundhouse. It, like the station, was demolished sometime in the late 50's or early 60's. Most all of the "old timers" like my daddy who worked for the MP are gone and so are the buildings.

Because of the roundhouse playing its roll in turning around locomotives, it aided the comfort in riding a passenger train. It was time for a change as an era of glamour emerged. Art deco appeared. A Screaming Eagle motif emblazoned on the front, with massive wings sweeping down the sides of the locomotives, captured our attention. Luxurious seats, dining cars and sleepers intrigued us. We saw women dressed to the nines or wrapped in furs or fox stoles. Men wore wide lapelled jackets, ties with diamond studded stick pins and wing tipped shoes and hats.

We won't see these things any longer. As we

shoved our minds and bodies into the new frontier, aka, space age, we erased the past and fast … faster we flew, higher and higher we went … away from a rousing era of trains and romance of the rails.

VIRTUAL REALITY SITCOM

Leave It to Beaver was a classic down home television show. No foul words ever entered the dialogue and it always had a happy, drive on a point ending. There were four people in this all American, apple pie, non dysfunctional, perfectly formed toothed, sit down to dinner, supposed middle class family. June Cleaver managed to be a stay at home mother with the cleanest house in the country. She smiled a lot in a melancholy way but had no female "voice". It was as though she waited for her husband to tell her it was okay to talk. That was wimpy. Her hair was never out of place and her apron was clean.

Did she ever do laundry? I saw her carry a laundry basket but it only contained towels. Maybe I missed the shows with grungy, smelly clothing. I never saw her get down on her knees to scrub baseboards but I did see her with a dust cloth. That dust had to go somewhere but apparently it didn't adhere to ceiling fan blades. Movie sets don't have ceilings but they have plenty of walls. I wonder if those neatly manicured nails rummaged through window sills to retrieve any tiny pieces of lost toys or record player needles. Did she drive a car or was there not time enough in those thirty minute segments to show her behind the wheel. She must not have grocery shopped because I always saw her husband, Ward, bring in a sack of groceries. One sack but then, in the 50's a sack of food lasted a week. Apparently they had plenty to eat because June's stove was going full bore.

Ward Cleaver was the bread winner, husband and father who toted a brief case. It seems, in most of the episodes, the only time you saw him was when he was leaving for work or coming home. A few, at home Saturday shows aired, but Ward seemed out of sync, lost in a world of "how did I get here, I am supposed to be at work?" Ward's absence was when Beaver, Wally or their friends were the most active doing most things normal kids do to get into trouble. On occasion, Ward's scowl made his brow wrinkle and an unharmonious screech emanated from his throat. Not once, did I see this man, dressed to the nines, come unhinged or be smeared with lawnmower grease.

However, there were attempts to show his manly duties with an occasional disheveled appearance. What was he doing? He never brought a leaky oil filter through the kitchen or yell for a rag to wipe his hands. No grime ever saw the underpinnings of this man's fingernails. His dirty socks didn't lie on the floor and his newspapers were neatly folded. He put his dirty coffee mug in the sink but never put salve on a burn from Fourth of July accidents. What in thunder is with this man? He is not normal.

The boys, Wally and Beaver, were the epitome of childhood greatness. They had fights, albeit, neither one of them appeared harmed. They climbed out of windows, stomped through mud puddles, lost clothing at school and hid half eaten food under the bed. You could catch them drink out of wax carton milk containers and sling peanut buttered knives on the counter. Sometimes a black eye found its way to another person's fist but it didn't hinge on alcoholic beverages. They were simple disagreements between children whose temperaments got in the way. Loud music didn't rock the house with amplifications of earthquake magnitude. The "scripted" boys were loving and thoughtful to one another. They were being paid to be kind. This show was a good thing as it depicted how all families hoped they could be. One in spirit with a willingness to grow into adult, let's sit down and discuss the problem family. It was good but not reality.

My household was different from the Beaver family. I had a voice and said my say regardless of who disliked what they heard. Never in my motherhood did I prance around with a clean apron. My hair was not always coifed early in the morning. In fact, I was told if I was ever kidnapped, at the first ray of light I would be set free. I would either talk them to death or scare the wits out of them. Name your poison!

Believe me; I could scrub baseboards, clean closets, floors and ceiling fan blades until my house shined. The minute the kids got home from school, it was back to square one as three small tornados swept through with a vengeance. For a long while, our house with many kids raiding cabinets, refrigerators and deep freeze for their continual hungry bottomless pits kept that one bag of groceries pleading for mercy. That is why we had a garden and I canned so much food.

My washing machine and dryer didn't have an off button. I fed the electric and gas company employees for years. They were proud to see those bonuses because of the Rapier insanity. My hands and fingernails dug down air-conditioning vents to extract wayward pieces of jigsaw puzzles, lost G.I Joe gear and doll clothes. I have chased critters out of the house, shooed away tarantulas, pulled a ferret out of the couch, fed and cleaned out cages of guinea pigs, hamsters and gerbils until I was blue in the face. My carpet and I coldly embraced oil slicks from installations of racing clutches, brakes and drippy oil filters. My husband didn't sit on his laurels with clean fingernails, either. Before he tamed our little acre, he wore out four lawnmowers because of the abundance of rocks on this mountain, trailed in enough grass clippings to stuff a queen-size mattress and patched bicycle tubes by the dozens. After the kids grew up, much to their chagrin, they had to mow the lawn. I constantly heard "no, it's your turn." Lava soap melted as fast as the wrapper was opened. Yes, we all screamed, had ring tailed tooter fits and threatened bodily harm because we were the actual normal, all American, apple pie, had Fourth of July displays, dysfunctional, non-perfect toothed, sit down to dinner, middle class five person family.

Perfect like the Cleaver's sitcom? No, but I wouldn't change a thing because we were in the midst of a non-pay virtual reality show.

PORCH SWINGS

Wood plank porches adorn many houses. Even caves with overhanging rocks provide shelter and refuge from storms. The Latin word, porticus, and Greek portico are where we get the word porch. Although the 18th century had a few porches they didn't come into true fashion until the Victorian times. Wrap around verandas with overhangs swept the massive houses. What made them need the oversized porches? Maybe it was a need to keep in touch with prosperous times as industry gained in popularity. Now that they had a porch, they needed somewhere to sit. I suppose those people used straight back kitchen chairs or hauled an old sofa to the front porch. Porches were a gathering place to watch the simplest thing. Perhaps the view was small children at play as they invented games to keep their minds sharp. It might have been where a beau wooed his chosen one. People used porches to entertain their neighbors or lull away their time from a hard day's work.

It's now the 50's, an era to carry on the Victorian porch and its whims. Every year it was the same scenario. An August, long, lazy summer's month was upon us. Everyone knew not a breeze would stir the sticky atmosphere around us but there was hope. We were aware the humid temperature was going to hug the air stifling the urge to venture outside but then

SKIPPING DOWN MEMORY LANE

again, there was a remedy. It was natural to think clothes would cling to the body as that of sticky plastic wrap trapped inside a sauna. Yet, there was a way to satisfy and soothe a weary body.

It was long before television shattered a peaceful existence and air conditioning to acclimate our bodies to frigid temps. If you were able, you might afford an oscillating fan to ward off brow sweat but all of us were accustomed to living a simple life. We watched as some men worked hard in the noon day sun while children romped on dying grassy knolls without a care in the world. Women went about their household chores as the majority of them were stay at home moms. Daytime was rife with hard work but, come sunset, the front porch and its magical porch swing came alive.

Every evening, people could be seen on their front porches. People waved to their neighbors or invited them to join in on conversation. Their comfort, even though it was ghastly hot, would be found in a porch swing. For them, it was not a wooden swing attached to the ceiling with chains, it was a friend. A repetitious, swish, swish could be heard as they kicked the floor with one foot to insure the swing continued to send them into a peaceful state of mind. It was a soothing sensation, a heart slowing calm pace.

A gentle breeze, picked up from the swaying swing, was our hope and remedy. Usually, a tall glass of fresh perked iced tea perched atop one leg as the condensation dripped its cool. On occasion, a person might swipe the forehead with the icy cold drinking glass. It was the norm until the dark of night crept its way upon the porch sending people back into the house. The porch swing would have to wait until the next sunset. Once again, the heat of day found its way inside. Some people dashed their beds with water by using the old fashion sprinkling bottle used to dampen an ironing load. More often than not, paper fans, made from pages of a Sears Roebuck Catalog, swiped the air to mimic the swaying porch swing breeze.

Have you recently looked through old photographs? How many of them were taken with a porch in its background? Was Grandma or Grandpa sitting together in a swing? Maybe Grandpa was whittling a piece of wood making mounds of shavings on the front porch planks. Was there a spot in any picture where snuff or tobacco found its way to the edge of the porch? How about the antics of children? Were they captured on film, pushing the envelope of a too high swing, sometimes dislodging the chain from its hook? Did your honey court you on the front porch or sit in a swing with you, whispering sweet nothings in your ear? It seems the front porch and swing were the precursor to a game or family room. Everyone enjoyed quality time on a front porch and took the time to invite neighbors to sit a spell or have a chew. Back then, porches and porch swings were the personification of everyday life.

What happened? What we knew to be a simple life is now complex. It seems things come and go in our own self indulgent harried world. We turn down the AC to avoid going outside and grab a soft drink to guzzle while we kick back and prop our feet on a luxurious recliner. Instant or bottled tea has taken the place of fresh perked and no ice cubes clank together inside a drinking glass. We are not happy if condensation drips on our clothes. Taking a Kodak picture of friends sitting on a front porch swing is no longer important nor is the conversation. Big fancy houses don't have front porches as it would be invasive or tacky to have the gentle porch swing friend as a permanent guest. Are swings and porches passé or do we consider them too country or undignified for our life styles? Whatever the case, I don't think any one of us would want to go back in time to relive what we call "the good old days" nor will we swish, swish the front porch planks trying to stir up a gentle breeze with a porch swing.

Back then, I considered us to be very lucky ... lucky to have neighbors who shared time with one another. Listening to the clank of ice cubes while sitting on a porch swing and laughing in spite of the heat, was one of life's greatest pleasures. Such is life but if any of you have a porch, I hope you don't forget the dear old swinging friend. As you clink your ice tea and sway back and forth, will you please let me know if you helped the swing find its breeze?

TAKE ME OUT TO THE BALLGAME

If I asked you who was on the box of Cracker Jacks, without peeking or running out to buy the yummy treat, could you describe the mascots? What is the stance and is there anything in the hands or are they empty? Would you know what color the mascot is wearing and what is at his feet? You know you know the answer and it's on the tip of your tongue but it's illusive. Who produces the product?

Cracker Jacks is one of the most popular snacks sold since its inception. It wasn't always called Cracker Jacks. In 1893 when the World's Fair was in Chicago, an entrepreneurial gentleman decided to sell his concoction of molasses, popcorn and peanuts to fair goers. It was sold as candied popcorn and peanuts and it clumped together as chewy bits. It took a couple of years to figure out how to mass produce it so the product wouldn't stick together. Brothers, William and Louis Rueckheim, devised a way make individual pieces of goodies. They figured out, that adding oil to each batch they made inside a drum like a cement mixer, made the product better. When an excited taster dubbed it "that's crackerjack" the founders had the name for their product. It was a solid name and a trademark ... Cracker Jacks.

A wax sealed package was designed by Henry Gottlieb Eckstein to ensure freshness. It was called the "Eckstein Triple Proof Package" because it kept out germs, dust and moisture. It was so successful in keeping the product fresh, the company re-organized under Rueckheim Bros. & Eckstein. The year 1908 brought Cracker Jacks to "high in the sky, as American as apple pie" fame as it was given free publicity through the nationally known Tin Pan Alley song *Take Me Out to the Ball Game*. At one time, in 1858, the song was called *The Base Ball Polka* but that was before baseball was what we know today. Given the opportunity to hawk peanuts, popcorn and molasses together in a single box, what better way could the snack be known to the public than through baseball games? It was a class act for the Rueckheim Brothers and a boon to their product.

Prizes of little value could be found in the Cracker Jacks box. It started in 1912 when the illustrious duo decided to secret pieces of trinkets to surprise the people indulging in the favorite snack. It was a hit and the pop-culture slogan "came in a Cracker Jacks box" took the public by storm. The little gadgets or small toys didn't amount to anything but the buyers thought it was a novel idea. Later, pieces of puzzles and jokes replaced the toys and trinkets.

I remember picking through all the popcorn nuggets to find the surprise. Unfortunately, it was a tin soldier, plastic birds, Indians, goats, rabbits or small toy horns. There was nothing that interested me but I do suppose some of those trinkets might be considered antique and perhaps more valuable than I realized as a child. Only one time in all the years I purchased a box of Cracker Jacks did I find a girls tin ring with a plastic gem. The gem was green with oversized prongs holding it down. I had to mash the tin round to fit my finger and in the process it made square. It pinched my finger, snagged my clothes and found its way to the trash bin. It's too bad I didn't have the foresight to keep it as it would be a vintage collectable. What was so maddening was that all the prizes were at the bottom of the box. You either ate all the Cracker Jacks at once or crushed the box and Cracker Jacks to get to the prize.

The mascots, Sailor Jack, in his blue uniform and white hat perched atop his head and his dog, Bingo, began to grace the identifiable box in 1918. The trademark logo of this pair didn't happen until a year later. Today, they are still adorning the box with the familiar stance but not in the traditional colors. Sailor Jack is in a bright blue suit instead of the denim color I knew as a child. The box has taken on a different format. Instead of being several ounces in a large box, one box is reduced to a little over one ounce content. I noticed you can buy three boxes for ninety-nine cents making the contents a tad over three ounces.

The original box had the words "Toy Surprise Inside" at the top of the box in the same denim color. Today, it's gone and above the banner hails the words "0 grams of trans fat." On a white baseball, the words "Toy Surprise" are replaced with big yellow letters. Other formats have taken hold as well with Sailor Jack and Bingo not as prominent on the outside. If the box gets any smaller, the mascots will disappear all together.

Things change as the years go by and Cracker Jacks is no exception. In 1964, after the heyday of my spending spree of munching Cracker Jacks, the company was bought out by Borden in a bidding war with Frito Lay. In 1997, Frito Lay became the owner of Cracker Jacks. While the box has changed in colors and layout, Sailor Jack and his dog, Bingo, has a story to tell. Still young as ever with not a gray hair in his head, Sailor Jack still salutes the public while he and Bingo entices all to enjoy a box of Cracker Jacks.

I hope the two of them stay around for a very long time while everyone plays baseball and sings, *Take Me Out to the Ball Game*.

TIS – TAIN'T

Webster comes in all sizes. Those that come to mind are the pocket for the person who needs a word in an instant, desk for those secretaries who want the boss to know they want all documents to be correct with spelling and library to pretend it's an intellectual search. Definitions, in my generation, were exactly what were printed. They listed all sorts of things such as synonyms, history, how to pronounce the word and derivation. Some dictionaries came with language translations but putting the tongue around the pronunciation was difficult. A body could skew a word or misconstrue the proper definition if not careful. Dictionaries were easy to tote around and didn't take a tackle and wench to lift it off a table.

We made up words to pretend we knew what we were saying but some word archivist would call us on the carpet and bring us down a notch or two. Most times the person was an uppity, proper speaking English major and we didn't have a clue what they were saying. Kids in my day didn't even know what the term English major meant or cared why they were noted for their correct diction. We talked 'Arkansaw' with a few naries, ain'ts, twern't, reckontwus, how'djaknow, didjacatcheny, gonnagitawhuppin and other run together words. Our language was pure country and everyone knew what we meant. The words we spoke were not in any dictionary and even if they were we didn't know how to spell them. How could we possibly look them up in Webster? Webster would have rolled over in the grave trying to put a definition to our speech.

I don't know how many words are in a dictionary and quite frankly, I don't give a hoot. It's not in my "bucket list" to count them. Some are ten dollar words and others a mere cent. In other words, why use a ten dollar word when a penny word will fit the bill? One thing I know for certain, the words we used in my day don't have the same meaning. Today, Webster would weigh 1,500 pounds or more if word-hoarders put their heads together and tallied up all the definitions for a single 'Arkansaw' word. All I know is that if people in our area who speak 'hill' talk were allowed to sit in on compiling a dictionary it would gum up intellectual brains and have them flubbing their lips.

A few of my all time favorite words and their meanings are: AINT – your aunt or AIN'T – won't do anything, AIGS – something you eat for breakfast, ARNJ – An orange or a fruit, AST – ask something, AT – (that) old thing ain't worth a flip, BAIGGED – begged, BARRER – someone who borrows something, BOBBED WAR – barbed wire, BRAINCH – a stream, CHAW or BAKKE – tobacco, CHUR – go cheer up that sad old fellow, CIPHER – do math, CURSEEN – kerosene, DAINCE – do a two step, DUMLAR – liar, ET – ate, FARMAN – fireman, FRASH – something new, FURRINER – foreign person, GIT-A-LONG- lower back, GOODERN – good person, HEERED – heard something, HIDYDO – hello, IFFIN – could be or if you take a mind to do something, IGNERNT – dumb person, INJUN – Indian or car engine, KINELY – maybe or thank you, NELLAR – vanilla, NEWMONIE – pneumonia, OBIDDY – nosy old woman, PEENCHED – pinched, PILLER – pillow, PLAK – play like, PURTY – pretty, PURTNEER – nearly, RAHCHEER – right here, REVNOOERS – gun toting still smashers, TIS – it's, RITELY – could be so, RURINT – ruined, SARR – sour, SHURFF – sheriff, SMARTS – hurts, THANG – thing, TAINT – is not, TOWK – talk, TUMPT – to fall over, TWIXTWEEN – between something, UNJUN – onion, VITROLIE – record player, WALLEYED – nuts, crazy, loco, WHOOP'NHOLLER – a bit far away, WORSH – wash.

Those words may seem out of the ordinary and sound cockeyed but they aren't. Where we live, in these beautiful Ozarks, people are accustomed to speaking with a specific dialect. When we speak, most of us drop the 'g' on words such as talking, doing, etc. We end those words with an 'i''. It's not any different from those living in other parts of the world or a language we can't understand. Hill talk is fascinating and musical and hinges on the poetic. I use some of those words every day of my life and wonder if I should be living somewhere on the north forty, growing my hair to my waist and wearing a granny dress and clog shoes.

Hillbilly is a word I embrace because it's a part of my heritage. Speaking the drawl and listening to someone doing likewise makes me know that person is from 'Arkansaw' or a close proximity. I say this because during our statehood, two Arkansas U.S. senators were going tooth and nail and battling it out (sounds familiar) over who was right and who was wrong. One was introduced as a senator from ARkanSAW and the other from Ar-KANSAS and it caused a hullabaloo. They were divided in how to spell and pronounce the word Arkansas. It was not until 1881 that a resolution was passed stating it should be spelled Arkansas but pronounced Arkansaw.

Since those two senators apparently didn't use a dictionary or couldn't spell worth a flip and phonics made them question each other's dialect, I have to question if they should have been senators. I can only imagine how Webster felt when he was defining the word Arkansas. So, I figure people can danged well talk the way they want to talk and throw the dictionary out the window. Even though I know Webster and try to speak and write properly, you can jist call me a hillbilly cuz I am an Arkansawyer frum 'Arkansaw' and proud of it!

TWIN CITY BUS

The other day, Dan was at Jack's Motor Company talking to Johnny Jack and other men who visit regularly. Johnny wanted to know if I had ever written about the bus line connecting Van Buren and Fort Smith, Arkansas. Yes, I have but more memories are angled inside a portion of my brain and the snapshot I see is vast. A person in the 50's and 60's depended on the diesel belching, black and white rear engine bus.

The front of the bus was flatter than a flitter and I often thought if the driver slammed the brakes; the back of the bus would flip over the front. The bus's brownish-black seats usually had slits in them and pieces of the cut interior would ram the back side of the passenger. Most women would lower the top portion of the windows while kids raised the bottom. Lowering the top prevented a woman's hair from blowing in the breeze because the early part of the 50's didn't offer too many varieties of hairspray. Move over, soft curls ... things are about to change.

In 1955, Helene Curtis offered women a product called Spray Net. From then on hair has been teased, straightened, curled, frizzed, bouffant ... enough hair in that stiff do to knit a sweater or shave it off and use it as a helmet, Afro, braided, permed or kinked, crimped, ironed, snip-dingle or corn rows (Movie: TEN), instant freeze, added to and taken out. With the advent of so many different hair spray lacquers a

SKIPPING DOWN MEMORY LANE

woman could roll down a window, stick her head out, pull it in an hour later and a single strand of hair wouldn't be out of place. Women, after spraying the hair in the late 50's & 60's walked around like zombies afraid to move any part of the body in fear of messing their "do." Hair turned from a silky mane to a stiff shoe brush. After these hair products appeared, women riding the bus didn't care what type of gale force winds whistled through the windows. They were wind proof.

My cousin Ann and I would synchronize time but it wasn't by a watch. We knew the bus route time and met each other at the bus stop near the viaduct of the old 64-71 Highway going across the Arkansas River Bridge. We would pay our token and ride to the roller rink on midland. It was in the general vicinity of where the defunct Wal-Mart is today and cattycornered from Harding Glass Factory.

The roller rink had kids lined up around the windows, hanging on to rails and trying to stand upright on four wheels. Air conditioning was unheard of as the rink had roll up, tarpaulin shades and the wood floors were always dusty. You could rent white or black shin high lace up shoes with rollers made of wood. They were opposite of those made of key adjustable metal, attach to your shoes, sidewalk rollers skates. On a Saturday, kids showed off the latest move or as a group doing a whip lash. The poor soul at the end of the whip most often screamed as their body flailed across the rink. They played music and offered couples a chance to win the best costume and dance routine. Unfortunately, the roller rink turned bowling alley and the bus ride we took stopped at the same corner but for a different kind of adventure.

This time we carried one piece swim suits, a towel and swim cap decorated with bright colored flowers. We thought we were the cat's meow. Getting off the bus at Harding Glass, I always looked at the mound of crushed glass. Sometimes when the sun hit the glass, millions of tiny rainbows glistened with gusto. The rainbows danced in the air daring anyone to touch their razor sharp beauty. It was breathtaking to see simple glass give off such radiance. Then, after watching the sun and its fancy, we walked down Kelley Highway a couple of blocks and then another two blocks to a swimming pool.

We headed past the bowling alley to Whittaker's swimming pool at 3420, North 31st Street. It was a two way street in a residential area with tree lined walkways. Whittaker's was a privately held pool but opened to the public for a nominal swimming fee. If a person was merely driving down the street, he/she wouldn't know the pool was there. However, I am sure the neighbors were aware of the boisterous kids splashing water. We had so much fun at Whittaker's but then; sometimes we went to Creekmore Park.

I was not too keen on switching busses so we got off the bus at downtown Fort Smith and walked to Creekmore Park. By the time we got to the park, we were so hot and tired the cool water was a wonderful relief. In desperation, we would leave the pool thirty minutes before we wanted to and then run like the dickens to catch the bus. It made me have nightmares. In my dreams it was very dark outside and the bus made its last stop at the Arkansas-Oklahoma Fair grounds. The driver was adamant telling me the bus couldn't make it any further. He stopped and I was the only one getting off the bus and I had to walk across the Arkansas River Bridge … alone. That is when I decided no more running to catch the bus … I stayed the heck away from Creekmore pool.

There were times the Twin City bus took us to downtown Fort Smith to window-shop. All of the fashionable department stores sat on the south side of Garrison Avenue and included Hunts, Penney's, Sears, The Boston Store and Mode-O-Day. I loved the bargain basement at the Boston Store but yet, the bargains didn't match my pocket book moths. The Mode-O-Day had reasonably priced clothing and for the most part, looked like the upscale merchandise.

As I made my first venture into the Mode-O-Day, my eye caught sight of a dress. It was so beautiful but I resisted and left it on the hanger. The thought of it burned my mind and I decided, if it was still there the following Saturday, I would purchase it. My heart sank when I went to the rack. It was gone. Lucky for me, the racks were moved to different positions in the store. The saleslady remembered me and directed me to the recent marked down rack. It was there. My first purchase from a Fort Smith department store was a yellow dress with a white Peter Pan collar, black leather belt and black shoulder shawl. The whole ensemble cost me a whopping $2.98 including tax. As I rode back home on the bus, I couldn't resist the temptation to open the twine wrapped package. I wanted to make sure the dress was inside, the one I chose as it waited on my purchase … it was special. I felt uptown in my selection but disgusted I had spent the money. Saving money back then (even now) is what I prefer but the little yellow dress had my name all over it.

Twin City Buses took me to heights that children of today will never experience. They won't smell the disgusting waft of diesel unless they are on a school bus, roller skate inside a dusty, portable, circus tent rink, experience the fun at Whittaker Pool, exchange buses or run like the dickens to catch one, have nightmares about busses, see the Harding Glass Factory in operation, shop on the up-scale busy avenue of Fort Smith or purchase a complete ensemble for $2.98. I wouldn't change those times for anything but one thing I did back then is not on my agenda today. I found out I don't need roller skates as the bazillion acorns all over my yard indicates I can't skate as well as I remember.

SKIPPING DOWN MEMORY LANE

WASHING MACHINES & OLD FASHION CANDY

For some reason, Mother never made candy unless it was cold or snowy outside. Her favorite was fudge and taffy. Her fudge was the old fashion kind not made with marshmallow crème. I would sit on a chair and watch as she carefully measured each ingredient. The bitter chocolate looked so inviting; it tempted me to spoon a mouthful. Although I am not one for plain chocolate, I couldn't resist a heaping teaspoon full of the aromatic brown powder. For anything to smell so tasty, it couldn't be bad, now could it?

As I placed the spoonful on my tongue and swallowed, it took a while before the bitterness engaged my brain. It was foul tasting stuff, that is, what stayed in my mouth. A wad of the putrid stuff stuck to my tonsils and created a sneezing and coughing episode. One sneeze exploded through my nostrils and the result wasn't pleasant. My face looked as though I had wallowed in a mud puddle. The clothes I was wearing bore streaks of chocolate and I had to clean up the awful mess. It was the last time I ate plain Hershey's cocoa powder. Even though Mother knew best, she left me to experience what she told me not to do. It was one of those things kids do, thinking it won't hurt them to push the envelope. Hindsight is twenty-twenty after you do what you are not supposed to do and realize Mother or Daddy already traveled down that same road. They spoke with genuine experience.

When the chocolate candy was nearly at the soft stage, Mother would dip a spoon into the mixture. At an angle, if the chocolate dripped from the edge of the spoon in two slow droplets, it was time to let the candy set until it was time to beat. It was hard to keep from dipping a finger or two into the delectable mixture but I waited. Now the chocolate was shiny and cool, ready to beat until the luster faded into a dull mass. Hand beating the mixture was a chore as an electric mixer didn't exist in our household. Even though the wrist ached and muscles in the arms writhed in pain, once the beating started, you couldn't stop. She let me push the chocolate on to a buttered pan. I can remember her words. "Push the chocolate and don't scrape the pan. If you scrape, sugar crystals will form in the fudge." Every time I make homemade, old fashioned fudge, I am reminded of Mother's gentle words.

Another candy was salt water taffy. Matlock's Grocery store sold long slabs of taffy wrapped in dull colored wax paper. Mother figured she could make the same type of candy but she needed a good recipe. She trekked across the street to talk to Mattie West but Mattie didn't have the recipe. In desperation, Mother decided to concoct her own. She knew it was sugar, corn starch, corn syrup, water, margarine and salt. How much of each, she didn't know. Trial and error was the name of the game. She adapted the fudge recipe to suit her needs, sans chocolate. Oh boy, what a mess! The first batch was too gooey and as we pulled the "almost" ready taffy, it drooped and sagged like a worn out nag. We had sticky taffy in our hair, on our clothes and all over the kitchen. It wouldn't pull worth squat and it tasted too salty. Out it went and another batch of taffy was in the making. Reduce this, alter that, add a pinch and omit. This little scenario went on for a week until Mother hit the right proportions of each ingredient. After she piled the cooked candy on a large platter, it cooled enough to dip our hands into the gooey stuff. It was time to pull the taffy. We had no clue how long it would take but soon found out. Pull, fold, pull, fold, twist, tug took at least an hour. The candy began to lighten its shade and became shiny with a satin sheen. It would no longer take another pull or fold. Out came the scissor and Mother snipped the candy into strips like the taffy sold n Matlock's Grocery Store. It was delicious and Mother triumphed in her recipe and in another sneaky way.

Fast forward many years later. It was cold and snowy outside and my kids were out of school for the Christmas holidays. They were bored senseless because each consecutive Wednesday it snowed. The television blared from one cartoon to another and when their bedroom doors were closed, they were either plotting or fighting. They were not happy campers. Cold from staying outside too long sliding and tromping in knee deep snow made for exasperating moments of this harried mother. My washer and clothes dryer was on at full blast, non-stop with kids' wet clothes. They had to temporarily stay indoors.

What to do to appease kids? Taffy! It was Mother's recipe coming to the rescue. As we pulled and tugged at the taffy, it drained the excess energy from the kids. Their arms didn't have enough strength to inflict another blow. Thank goodness for Mother's recipe as it allowed me to hear laughter from rambunctious kids. The indoor fun lasted a couple of hours and I enjoyed the togetherness we shared. They were spent for a little while ... until the sugar rush plowed through them. Then, it was back outside with taffy shoved inside pockets for an extra boost of energy when hunger struck.

Mother was smart. I realized she made candy to keep me indoors on those inclement days. She had an old wringer washing machine and had to heat water to wash clothes. A clothes line was her dryer. I should have paid closer attention to her subtle gestures, as on our snowy days, I could swear my washer and clothes dryer had eaten Mother's taffy ... their energy was going full throttle.

SKIPPING DOWN MEMORY LANE

WHO WOULD'A THUNK IT?

It doesn't seem too far in the rear-view mirror but as I look over my shoulder, the years are mounting and fading in the distance. Forty or fifty years ago – gosh, when a body says it out loud, it's longer than one might expect. Quite a few things have changed but are they for the better? If you are my age, tell me if you remember any of these things and we will compare notes.

If I say black and white what comes to mind? If I say Lone Ranger, Mouseketeers, or Batman and Robin would you think mask, big eared hat or cape? If its fuzzy black and white would you think television? The only way you could clear the picture was to jiggle rabbit ears and then it didn't always work. Most times the 'snow' made black things white. These and other black and white classic re-runs are for the choosing but the rabbit ears we knew are only on live critters. Some people may have the two pronged, silver snow chaser somewhere in an attic but they are not good for anything and not valuable since so many were made. Remember the tin foil decorating the tips of the rabbit ears? It was supposed to help get better reception but all it did was fall off when you moved the ears. What about the size of televisions. They used to be small and now they are so gargantuan you have to sit outside to enjoy the super sized screens so the actors won't jump into your lap. I say we have been 'ized...hypnotized by the remote control and we idolize the TV.

Almost everyone likes chicken. Dan, my better half, and I like to watch Chopped on the food channel. It's a cooking show made up of four contestants using weird food contents inside a basket. They have to prepare an appetizer, entrée and dessert within an allotted time and use every ingredient in the basket. The judges are renowned restaurant owners or gourmet cooks. When food is prepared, if it doesn't meet the criteria, a contestant is chopped from the show. One episodes basket's content was chicken. The contestants prepared the food but one person failed to do the three 'P's'…prior, proper, planning. I knew what she did wrong and she did too, but it was too late. Her faux pas was using the same cutting board and leaving germs to swarm and contaminate other foods.

That contestant didn't have anything on me or Alma Peevey Parker. She and I beat her to the punch in being "chopped." In the seventies when we moved to Mt. Vista, our neighbor, Alma, asked if I would like some chicken. Sure I did but I didn't know what it entailed. Much to my surprise, when I looked out the back door toward her cleaned out dog pen, there was at least 100 live chickens ready for us to slaughter. Ye Gods and little bitty fishes! Beside the pen was a fire with a cauldron full of boiling water. Yep, you guessed it. We killed, plucked, gutted, singed pin feathers and dunked them in the water to remove any remaining feathers. One by one, into large ice buckets the chickens remained until we finished the ordeal around 9:00 p.m. Cleaning up the cockeyed smarmy mess was the pits and I vowed never to do it again. In my opinion, once was enough. As I took my bounty into the house, chickens lay all over my cabinet. Every one of them wound up in my freezer to be eaten by my hungry growing children. I didn't use rubber gloves on those blasted chickens or chastised my kids for touching them because of germs. Yes, I thoroughly cleaned my cabinets and utensils but it was not like it is today. Now, if I even think of cooking chicken, rubber gloves and bleach are a part of my work space. With all the crazy germs floating around, they don't stand a chance…my kitchen is 'ized…sanitized.

Did you ever get a cut or gash on any part of your body? Most kids did and it was a routine thing to run to their mother for a dash of Merthiolate that contained mercury or mercurochrome that left a stain on the skin. Sometimes we doused the cut with kerosene or a splash of rubbing alcohol or whatever was handy in the medicine cabinet. Any of those medicinal old time topical ointments supposedly killed germs but I seriously doubt it. Most of them burned like fire and we thought the sting was killing infectious germs. Then, like clockwork, we ran outside for a dash of dirt as a Band-Aid. If we stepped on a rusted nail or got a thorn in our hand we watched for red streaks to appear on our skin. If nothing happened we went on about our business.

If an infection appeared, a wad of bacon or fatty meat was applied to draw out the poison. We all know that didn't work but back when, people tried all kinds of concoctions as a remedy. Even greasy cob webs were put on cuts and I have to admit, sometimes it actually worked. Going to the doctor meant walking to the doctor's office or calling a cab that took forever to get to your residence. Sometimes, if it was serious, the doctor would make a house call. Not any more as that went by the wayside many years ago. Then along came injections for just about any kind of ailment. Tetanus,

Polio vaccine…you name it and there was a shot for whatever crawled up your nose. With all those injections, we have been 'ized … immunized.

When I was a kid, who would'a thunk it? Nobody thought of germs or drive-in size TV's. Heck, I think all kids clomped around in mud and maybe ate a wad of dirt and sat ten inches away from the TV to see the show. The old time ways of thinking and doing things are passé. Today, we may be ostracized if we are not socialized from old time thinking, criticized for certain beliefs, hypnotized by space age gadgets, sanitized or sterilized to fight off germs and immunized until those germs we thought were eradicated are fighting back. Even germs don't give squat about us being civilized because they have gone super sized. Better watch it, you may be victimized or traumatized by your TV. It may be one of those desensitized germs in disguise. No doubt about it we have been 'ized!

WILL ROGERS

William Penn Adair "Will" Rogers was born November 4, 1879 and died on August 15, 1935 while on a flight to Alaska with aviator Wiley Post. He was only 55 years old when he died near Point Barrow, Alaska but had already made his mark on this earth by numerous talents and political beliefs. Even though he was an actor, in the Guinness Book of World Records for throwing three lassoes at once, an author of six books and an acclaimed syndicated columnist, it was his pundits against government actions that pushed him to great heights and made him a household name.

He was born in Oologah, Indian Territory, what we know today as Oklahoma. He was the youngest of eight children born to Clement Vann Rogers and Mary Schrimsher who were part Cherokee descent. He was buried in Los Angeles, California but in 1944, his wife, Betty, had him exhumed and moved to Claremore, Oklahoma where his museum, Will Rogers Memorial, was dedicated by President Franklin Roosevelt. This great man whose tagline was, "I never met a man I didn't like" made many people venture to Claremore, Oklahoma. Among those people were my family and me.

Back in the 50's Daddy had an old, standard, black Ford truck with a knob for an accelerator. Actually, the truck was manufactured with the small protuberance in the floor. The dimmer switch for the headlights was on the left, upper side of the floorboard. The push-pull knobs for headlights were stationed on the right side of the steering column. The small am radio, which had its own on and off knob tuner, was directly in the front of the middle passenger seat. Unfortunately, anyone sitting there had to straddle the floorboard gear shift. Anyone with long legs might be whacked with the shifting mechanism. There were no seatbelts to keep you securely in place but the scratchy Velcro type seats stuck to your rear end and pant legs. It was almost like being plastered with glue, not to mention hotter than hells fiery furnace in the heat of summer. In order to put down windows, a crank handle did the trick. Beside the small windows were crank out wing windows and as the wind hit the outside, it pushed air toward a passenger. It was not air conditioning but cool enough to dry sweat as it rolled from the brow. Everything on the truck was manual. Small fuses to run the radio, windshield wipers and lights were housed in a trap door container beneath the steering wheel.

To manhandle the truck took finesse as the gargantuan, black, one position, in your face steering wheel took up a lot of space. The glove box was in front of the passenger seat and it didn't contain air bags. It took up most of the space on the dash board but housed necessary papers as well as two loaded pistols in their holsters.

Daddy decided we needed a vacation. He only told us we were going to Okmulgee, Oklahoma to see our Grandma Jones. She was my great-grandmother on Mother's side of the family. It turned out, everyone in the family wanted to go but how would everyone pile in the truck? A bit of ingenuity, on my daddy's part, settled the question. He built a camper to fit the bed of the truck. It jutted several feet into the air and looked like an outhouse. The only thing it didn't have was a chimney. It had narrow windows on each side and a fan out window at the rear. In order not to be suffocated with exhaust fumes, the windows had to be open at all times. He took an old twin mattress, cut it in half and made padded seats over the wheel wells. Another full mattress was fitted on the bed of the truck. It allowed for easy sitting or sleeping if all us kids got tired. Included in this outing was Grandma Hawkins, her sons, Raymond and John, Ruth (John's wife), their children Bea and John, Mother, Daddy (the driver), my sister and me. Four kids and all those adults crammed inside one truck made for some interesting conversations and choice words. We left at night so the hot sun's temperature wouldn't bake us to death in the cramped quarters. It was a long drive to Okmulgee as there was no interstate but plenty of dusty roads without roadside cafes or campsites.

Half way through the trip, I managed to sit or should I say, lay between two adults in the cab of the truck. All of a sudden, we came to an abrupt halt. The headlights on the truck went dead. We were somewhere between hot, dark and the bowels of hell. All the adults exited the truck trying to figure out what went wrong and how to fix it. Tempers were flaring like roman candles and I was told to keep my mouth shut ... they didn't need a little kid to do adult's work. However, I was the only one who knew what was wrong. If they had listened to me, we wouldn't have parked our butts on the side of the road for thirty minutes. Finally, I reached over, pulled "on" the headlights knob and watched as they stood in the beaming headlights like a bunch of blooming idiots. In my haste to settle in the front seat, I hit the knob turning off the lights. Needless to say, I sat upright the rest of the way to Grandma's house.

After our visit, the surprise was a trip to Claremore to visit the Will Rogers Memorial. At the time, I had no idea who he was or why we were there. The museum was magnificent with an array of souvenirs eager to jump into small hands. My selection was a small, sawdust filled doll costing one dollar. It was an Indian squaw with a papoose on her back. As we made our way through the museum, all the adults became somber. I watched as handkerchiefs wiped tears from eyes, as an icon of their generation could only be remembered through pictures and relics. There would be no more quotes or jabs at political figures from this great man named Will Rogers. For years after the world mourned his death, he didn't know it but one of his quotes would resound prophetic. "You must judge a man's greatness by how much he will be missed."

HEROES AND CHRISTMAS

This day, December 16, 2009, marks the sixty-fifth anniversary of the Battle of the Bulge. In 1944 near the end of World War II, the battle began raging in the mountainous region of Belgium and France near the western front of Luxembourg, Germany. The French called it Bataille des Ardennes. Germany referred to it as Unternehmen *Wacht am Rhein.* In English the term meant "Operation on the Rhine" referring to the patriotic German hymn titled, *Die Wacht am Rhine*. The U.S. Army's official name for the defensive was Ardennes-Alsace campaign but the English speaking people called it the Battle of the Bulge.

The "bulge" was a defensive action set forth by the Germans to split the American and British forces in half. Their ploy was to capture Belgium and Antwerp and then annihilate four allied armies, including American soldiers. It was the German's desire to force a peace treaty called the Axis Power. Our allied defensive tactics didn't prove favorable as communications, aerial reconnaissance, overconfidence and a host of other barriers caught them by surprise. It was bitterly cold and snow was so deep, the white out caused our air forces to be grounded. Men were surrounded by waist high snow. Cold and wet, shoes coming apart at the seams, socks frozen to the feet, outer wear not replaceable and scarce food surely was a source of undeniable anguish.

It was near Christmas, a time for family gatherings, good food and happiness.

Our soldiers and allies, far away from those they loved, were in a world of fear and chaos. The German offensive didn't come to fruition as planned. The defensive armies, even with horrible surroundings and suffering frostbitten bodies, managed to overwhelm the German army. German equipment was severely damaged and men surviving the bloody carnage retreated to the defensive Siegfried Line. The Battle of the Bulge was considered the bloodiest and single largest battle of World War II. Out of the 800,000 plus soldiers deployed to this battle, over 19,000 American soldiers were killed and casualties amounted to over 100,000. The Battle of the Bulge ended on January, 25, 1945.

Many years later, I found out my father-in-law, Paul Rapier, (I called him Pappy) was one of the soldiers fighting in the Battle of the Bulge. He was 32 years old when he entered the armed forces, married and had four children. At age 33, he was one of the lucky soldiers returning to American soil. He never spoke of the war but the expression on his face made us realize his world had been turned upside down. He was wounded in December 1944 and again in March of 1945. He was a recipient of two Purple Hearts and other distinguishing medals.

Most winter days Pappy would be sitting in his man chair near the fireplace. A half chewed stogie dangled from the right side of his mouth. Camel cigarettes lay nearby. His feet were almost inside the chimney as they were frostbitten and gray from plodding through freezing elements of the war. We would sit near him, rubbing his numb and prickly feet. Sometimes he would ask us to use sandpaper to help return circulation to the soles of his feet. The pain didn't subside, but with our caressing hands it helped soothe his gentle soul.

Christmas time was a blessed relief to him. I believe it was his way to escape the dark, gloomy and death defying time he spent in the war. His idea of a Christmas tree was out of the ordinary. He would traipse to the woods with grandchildren in tow, find the largest cedar tree, whack it down and haul it home. He made sure it was decorated with giant red, blue and green electric bulbs, bubbly candlestick ornaments and other assorted beauties. Silver tinsel dangled from every limb with the final adornment, an angel ... arms open wide perched at the top of the tree.

Every present was like candy canes, beautifully wrapped and addressed with his hand. Poinsettias were his favorite winter flower. It represented living things with its glorious red petals, as "blood" in its veins still pulsed. He never bought one at a time. Instead, his arms carried four or five. As he presented the Poinsettias to his wife, Naomi, his grin lit up the entire room. It was as though it was his way of saying 'I am alive' to the love of his life. The outside of their house on Loch Lomond had a single strand of multi-colored lights. The most impressive sight was a handcrafted, five-point star attached to the chimney. It dictated presence to those driving by the house and Pappy delighted in watching the cars slow in their approach.

Pappy was my hero ... a war hero and a hero to his entire family. He never ceased to amaze me. His ability to soothe a wounded soul and give a hand to those in need far surpassed the conflict and pain he endured. Today, as it was in 1944, military heroes abound keeping our country safe from harm. Many veteran heroes live in our town as they were among the brave soldiers fighting in the Battle of the Bulge and other engagements.

I think of all our heroes as the Poinsettia, the angel keeping guard and the star guiding everyone to safety. Now, it's time for Dan to put up the five-point, handcrafted star Pappy made in 1962. It's time for Pappy to light up our lives and yard with his radiant smile. Each brilliant bulb, as that of the North Star, represents the twinkle in his eyes and the childlike happiness he embraced at every Christmas season.

To all of you and to all the heroes who fought and still fight to make our Christmases special, I wish you a very Merry Christmas.

CONNECT THE DOTS

The most common word in the English language may be "the" but there are more words competing for the coveted award. Horrible little words rattling the minds of a mom or dad all over the world creep out of the mouths of a two year old. Babies are beautiful, a gift to hold dear and precious to the heart and we love to teach them words. Gibberish to our ears may be Ma-Ma or Da-Da but in reality, they are shortened words interacting with "maybe-maybe" or "don't-don't." They coo and smile and twist us around their little finger knowing full well they can make us do most anything. Parents are a bunch of wimps when it comes to babies and I am included in the wimp cycle. Mush is what you could call me. Pure mush and a push over!

Craning the ears to understand twaddle sentences emanating from a mouth full of razor sharp baby teeth, the pink matter between our ears nullifies common sense. We are eager to have a child talk, but then, when they do ... you can't make it stop. The words, "no, why, what, when, where, who, but, and how" are top examples overriding the word "the." I do believe, in order for a mother to keep her sanity, she devised schemes to thwart one-word sentences. They were in the form of games.

Do you remember the Quiet Game? It derived from the Quaker Game. "Quaker Meeting has begun. No more laughing, no more fun. If you show your teeth or tongue, you must pay a forfeit." Initiated from a rhyme, it turns into the quiet game where there is no smiling, laughing, frowning, moving or speech. If you squirmed in your chair, you lost the game. Most of the time if two or more children in a family played the game; it was a test of wills against the other. Can you imagine two children, in close proximity, keeping their mouths closed for an indefinite time? It won't happen because in desperation, one child will whack the other and the battle will begin. It's in the form of: she hit me to make me lose the game ... I couldn't help it, the chair tilted ... she stuck her tongue out at me. It's endless, as mouthy children won't sit or be silent for more than two seconds. It's humanly impossible. The Quiet Game turns into *Battlestar Galactica*, where one child is determined to do bodily harm to an opponent and the mother turns into Baltar trying to keep her colony intact.

Mother's are adept in finding other ways to keep the unending questions at bay. The game, I Spy, makes children be silent while searching for a mysterious object. It was popular long before Jean Marzollo and Walter Wick created the game board. It didn't involve playing cards or spinning boards to enhance a child's memory or motor skills. A mother usually looked around the room to select an item. It might be a thimble or other inanimate article. She might give a clue in that it was round, square or a color. When the child decided he / she knew the answer they screamed out I Spy. This game helped children learn the endless possibilities of animal, vegetable, mineral properties and expanded their vocabulary.

A long time ago, people didn't have access to reams of paper but we did have newspapers and paper grocery bags. Origami or folding paper to make simple or elaborate decorations was a favorite pastime and made kids concentrate. Simple paper hats, airplanes and making Christmas trees kept us occupied. Pencil and paper games were another silent victory for the mother. If a child was old enough to understand paper drawing in Connect the Dots, a picture came alive with simple straight lines. Coloring books could mesmerize a child as the crayons deposited their waxy colors on pictures.

Another thing to activate the mind of a child was magic rocks. The Five & Dime sold magic rocks by the dozens, as it was chemistry and science and enthralled little eyes as we waited patiently for them to grow. Depending on the size of container you used, these salt rocks, as you poured various coloring chemical agents atop them created a science project direct from *Jurassic Park*. The first day watching them didn't make them expand. However, the next day they turned into the most beautiful red, blue, green and yellow stalagmites. Delicate by nature, a simple touch to the container made them crumble into dust.

All of these games and projects aided a mother as a child grew from one stage to another. A child's one word, defiant barrage of questions didn't stop. It continued as we morphed into adults and engaged our minds as we journeyed through life by playing our own game of connecting the dots. Think about it, when you say, "No, why, what, when, who, where, but, and how."

Life and actions are unanswered questions!

DO YOU SEE WHAT I SEE?

Close your eyes. Do you see what I see? Not yet? Well, we better start travelling down the path and then I bet it will become clear. What did your small town look like when you were in your teens? For you guys, are you able to envision the town drag as you showed off your brand new white wall tires? How many of you left the blue on the tire so your friends would know you had been to a garage? Did you gut the muffler so a loud roar would emanate from the pipes? What about those twin mufflers or getting a ticket or warning for barking the tires? Has it become clearer? You wheeled your car doing a U-turn at the old water department as you and your girlfriend or load of boys scanned the area to see if someone was watching. No one got a ticket for doing a U because the police did the same thing. You were dragging the gut.

Do you remember your first check? If you are honest, I bet you wondered why your wages for a week didn't mesh with the hours you worked. Did you sit in the car looking at the check and do a quick cipher of the tally thinking your boss made a mistake. You pounded the steering wheel screaming. "What? This can't be right. I was planning to fix up my car! It will take me forever to save enough money." You worked too many hours for so little pay and your boss must be cheating you out of what was rightfully yours. How many of you were red faced and fuming as you marched back in the store demanding to know where the rest of the money was? "Taxes? You mean I have to pay taxes?" Taxes ... those dumb taxes ate away all those hard hours stocking grocery shelves or working in someone's detail shop.

Our school did teach accounting, talked about taxes and tried to help you learn the value of balancing a check book. Some listened and others turned a deaf ear. Don't feel bad, as kids of today are doing the same ... where is my money, you cheated me routine. Even today, high schools teach accounting (or should if they don't) but the first check for any kid blows their minds. It's a reality shock, a wakeup call to what life will be as an adult because taxes increase if you make more money ... yet you will still be in the same dumbfounded rut wondering where it all went. It's a vicious cycle to which none of us can escape. About now, are you wishing you had all the money you put into your 'wheels' or saying, "If I had a nickel for every dollar I spent, I would be rich."

For you gals, I bet you did the same thing but a lot of us didn't have our minds set on paychecks. It was about boys and their cars and our hair. Most girls didn't have a car because it wasn't necessary. Either a boyfriend or male acquaintance was eager to be seen with you because it put another notch on his "status quo." Sometimes it caused a ruckus with flapping lips. "Guess who I saw ... with ... you know who!" "What? I thought she was supposed to be going with so and so!" Whether they thought it was true or not, girls had a way of gossiping for the fun of it.

A clique of popular girls and jocks would gather near the brick bench by the gymnasium. Other groups of kids hung out together near the flagpole, sat on the wide concrete steps going into the building, or huddled together to have a quick 'not on the school grounds' smoke. Whenever someone saw a foot stomp or hands on the hips, it meant cat fur was about to fly. Whatever was said would, on occasion, bring out the cat claws, hissing and a few choice coined phrases. "Why, if she messes with him again, I'll jerk out all of that peroxide blonde's hair." "She doesn't know who she is jacking around. I'll give her a fist full."

For the most part, rumors were just that, rumors without one thread of truth but it made an exciting day for those who waited to see a bloodletting. Ninety-nine percent of the time, it was all smoke rings, a ruse of sorts to let the 'grapevine' wrap around the high school to see how fast the rumor would grow. It was a game for the kids to see how many teachers would come unhinged or stay on guard by looking over their shoulders.

However, right after the three o'clock bell, a couple of girls, on occasion, would live up to their barbed-wire tongue threats. A rumble was eminent. Near the railroad tracks beside the home economics building or out of sight behind the gym, they pounded the daylights out of each other. On those occurrences, our principal already heard the grapevine bell and could be seen shooting out the door near the office, running like a mad hatter to stop the fight. I don't know which was more stupid, two girls trying to emulate Sonny Liston or a refereeing principal taking a mid-section blow while grappling boxing wannabe's by the nape of the neck. The only thing coming out of these fights was a hair-do full of pebbles; raccoon eyes smeared with mascara and a principal making them listen to his rendition of his favorite royal song. "For the record, this is my playpen. It's my compulsion to give you expulsion. Don't you know that fighting makes me do my sidewinder wicked grin?"

After listening to the principal spout his play by play, thought provoking, life's enduring race to the finish line, the girls would agree to disagree. All is well that ends well? Not really. Because, every now and then those same girls would show up on school grounds with shiners, a cheek bone jutting out like a fresh plucked rosy plum or lips swelled so large, it would give those modern day injected lips a run for the money.

Baffles me why they would tell their friends how to keep a hair style if all they wanted to do was fight. They tossed and turned as the curler's wire prongs mashed the skull into the brain, woke up with a headache, and had wayward Bobbi pin imprints across the nostrils. If they managed to get through one day without a fight, the 'do' was wrapped in turban style toilet paper to show off the next day. It amounted to futile self-imposed pain. Another roll in gravel, over a boy who probably was not worth the effort, made their 'do', they tried to keep all day, look like a wicked witch having lost her broom in flight to a Macbeth, "Double, double toil and trouble; Fire burn, and cauldron bubble" convention.

Is it clear now? Were you able to look back to a time and place of your youth? Are you able to remember some of the things you did and see the towering gymnasium and brick wall where you sat waiting for the 8:00 bell? What about your conversations, bouffant hair-do's and fights? Do you see the yellow school busses by the shop building? Can you hear the mufflers rumble on your first car and if you do are you wishing for another drag the gut? I can still see those things, smell cafeteria food, and all the other wonderful things as time suspended it in my memory. Do you see what I see?

E.T. PHONE HOME

We know the universe is vast and our galaxy, The Milky Way, is not the only galaxy to grace the skies. According to the internet, the Milky Way contains possibly over 400 billion stars, massive dust particles and gases supporting our lives through the solar system. Wikipedia, the free encyclopedia, says our system is only one of the billions we can see with our naked eye. Scanning the skies, we pick up a fraction, maybe a dot the size of a pin prick. Actually, all we see is the portion of the sky in our view.

The way I see it, if I look at my body as a whole and see one small pore on my arm it's the Milky Way. Putting aside the tiny pore, the rest of my body, in cells, makes up the entire universe. It's mind boggling to know our earth might be compared to a tiny single cell. If we think of how many cells our bodies contain and the variety of complex sizes, it leaves us minuscule compared to the rest of the universe. Are we the only planet with life form?

I am a faithful reader of Ben Boulden's column, *Inquire Within* of the Times Record. He is articulate, has a distinct writing voice, sometimes funny, informed and refined to those who might question his answers. Thursday, November 5, he touched on a subject regarding the strange lights hovering above Van Buren. As he said, it was the summer of August 1966, and people were buzzing like bees about the bright lights zipping across the clear sky. It was out of the ordinary, a foreign sight unlike anything we had seen.

The night was hot in August but not any hotter than the usual summer evening. My husband, Dan, and I were outside sitting in lawn chairs unaware of the hoopla being raised by other people in Van Buren. We lived on North 24th Street one block north from J.J Izard School. Our house was nowhere close to the airport. As we looked into the night sky, right above our heads loomed seven perfectly shaped orbs. The center object was brilliant white and much larger than those surrounding its perimeter. Faint red and blue colors emanated from the six smaller orbs and they did appear as flashing strobe lights. The six circling objects were moving in sync with its counterpart.

To put it in perspective, the height of the objects was somewhat close to watching a low flying jet or a small aircraft. The orbs were not attached to any high-altitude jet. They were not too high or too low, and without question much larger than a danged old orange or pumpkin! There was no noise associated with those objects but they moved lightning fast. If you blinked, they moved into another position. At one point, they were above us. Then, they moved quickly to the west, to the north and south. As we watched them, the pattern they took was in straight lines. They were going straight up, straight down and straight forward. There was no jagged flight pattern. We thought they disappeared but soon enough, they hovered over us again. It was as though they couldn't figure out where they wanted to be. We watched as they zipped straight up toward the heavens. Like a flash, all of them, moving together as one, vanished.

SKIPPING DOWN MEMORY LANE

I do know in the summer of a year in the 50's it was so dry it was hard to breathe. Every blade of grass burned to a crisp. Mother and Daddy and other people searched the skies for clouds, praying for rain as crops were scorching in the daytime sun. The actual year eludes me but someone decided to sow seeds in the clouds to produce rain. There was speculation if it would create rain but since it was so dry, what would it hurt?

The "rain maker" was to fly his plane into the clouds and sow chemicals. Unfortunately, we had to wait to see if it worked. While we waited, the nights were so hot Mother and Daddy let my sister and me sleep outside on cots. We hoped for a slight breeze while we mopped our brows with a wet rag for relief. If the rainmaker did indeed sow seeds in the clouds, we didn't see strange lights in the sky as we lay there looking toward the heavens. Then, we weren't out there all night as the next morning we woke up looking at four walls instead of the sky. To my knowledge, though, no one reported sightings.

If Homer Berry, "the self-proclaimed Arkansas rainmaker" did scatter chemicals in the summer of 1966, did he inform the news media? Did he use frozen carbon dioxide by the components of silver iodide and dry ice? If we can put a man on the moon and bring them home safely, man a space station and blow a crater in the moon to find water, why is it not feasible aliens were here in 1966? Because we are a "pore" sized planet within a galaxy of the universe, who is to say we didn't see, in the summer of 1966, visitors from another planet? Funny isn't it, an officer from the Little Rock Air Force Base came here to investigate the sightings but news coverage "just happened to end" when Homer Berry, a retired Air Force Major laid claim to starting the whole shebang. Air Force ... hello!

For me, there is one little flaw in this theory. Without clouds on that hot summers' day and evening, if the seeds "supposedly" were planted around the state during the day would they not have fallen to the ground due to gravity? Why did other parts of the state not see these objects? Did all of those seeds take a poll and decide to wad up over Van Buren? Between me, thee and the gatepost ... Dan and I know what we saw and it sure as heck wasn't balled up orange or pumpkin sized chemical seeds. E.T. phone home!

SEVEN WONDERS

Seven Wonders of the World has included a multitude of architectural structures all over the world. From The Middle Ages to Modern times, people have selected sites they thought would be of interest to travelers of the world. How many of you have been to the traditional places? Have you seen the Leaning Tower of Pisa, the Great Pyramid of Giza in Egypt or trekked down the Grand Canyon? World traveler I am not so a metal detector won't be necessary, since I didn't lose anything in those areas. Today, other wonders have been added to this list, but alas, my list has not been included and they aren't man made. I wake up in a new world every day, see grand things and marvel at their beauty. Here are my seven wonders.

Trees are magnificent and stand the test of time even when hurt by catastrophic events. All of them send down their form of reproduction by seed or root system and sprout where you least expect to find them. It's their way of survival. They are alive, know when to burst forth with leaves, go dormant to endure a drought and can reveal their age with inner rings. Trees are a source used in constructing houses and housing our feathered friends. Trees are melodic in the rustling of leaves and give off a symphony when songbirds perch on the limbs. Most trees can heal themselves with burls and can put off new shoots when someone or something damages a limb. There are exceptions to this rule. Pine trees can't produce new shoots from a severed limb and the Aspens in Colorado are from a single seedling spread by root suckers. To me trees have considerable character with a might so strong no man could structure them. They take in our carbon dioxide as we exhale. It's said; one single mature tree can absorb carbon dioxide at a rate of 48 lbs. per year and release enough oxygen back into the atmosphere to support 2 human beings. Every person exhales nearly 2.3 tons of carbon dioxide per year. Imagine that ... one tree stores about thirteen pounds of our exhaled air per year! Magnificent wonder of the world.

If it weren't for trees, we wouldn't have oxygen. Can you see air or grab it with your hands? It's all around us and inside things but invisible to the naked eye. The only time we might think we see air is when small particles of dust whirl in front of us. It's our lifeline because without it we couldn't survive. Oxygen is a natural state and a wonder.

We all complain, at one time or another, that rain puts a damper on planned activities. Did you ever stop to think the rain provides growth? It's not manmade but given to us as part of our source for living. We need it for nourishment and to cleanse the air we breathe. Without rain, we would be a vast wasteland, void of life. Yet, it's not on the list of wonders.

Without the oxygen, water or light we wouldn't have prisms. Sure, we can turn on a lamp to have light, but only when bright, white sunlight hits an object or reflects through droplets of water do we get prisms or rainbows. Imagine going through life without a rainbow. The color wheel of a rainbow only shines when the sun casts its light through the lingering mist

SKIPPING DOWN MEMORY LANE

of a shower. A glass object, hit at a certain angle with the sun's rays, will project brilliant colors of violet, indigo, blue, green, red, yellow and orange, or wavelengths of color. Funny isn't it that only blue, red and green are true primary colors and are nature's own. Anything else we see is man's ability to cross breed species by combining shades to produce what we visualize. What's even more remarkable is when two colors, next to each other combine as one; it spreads the prism into incredible shades.

Birds are part of my seven wonders. It's pleasant to watch them and sometimes comical knowing they are almost parallel to humans in a routine. Non-predatory birds sleep at night while those out for blood prey on the defensive. They fight among themselves in territorial reign and peck at the weakest link. They coax fledglings from the nest in order for them to learn to live on their own. Some birds use their wits to lay eggs in another bird's nest so they won't have to take care of them. Blue birds are promiscuous and don't give a hoot about being monogamous. Mourning Doves mate for life. Crows steal young birds from their nests. Robins wait until birds peck the birdseed from the ground and then gather uncovered worms. Most birds migrate from one part of the country to another for climate change. It's true; birds of a feather flock together and are true wonders.

The human body and life, as I see it, is a wonder. Although "man made," we aren't constructed from concrete or put together with hammer and nails. No two bodies or minds are alike or perfect ... not even twins. Two people, seeing the same thing, will describe it differently. We might hear the same spoken words or read the same sentence but we have the ability to come to our own conclusion. It's a good thing because if everyone agreed on everything, then only one of us on this planet would be necessary. Our idea of agreeing would change in a heartbeat if told one of us had to leave this earth. Who would hold up their hand? It's the wonder of wonders.

Last but not lease in order of my seven wonders is how the earth sits in the universe, aided by the sun and moon. Placed on an axis, our beautiful world tilts and rotates but remains constant, providing us with the necessary elements for life. We stay grounded by means of gravity, enjoy the seasons of change and can be in awe at the beauty surrounding us. The world, as a whole, should be a wonder.

These are but a few on my list of Seven Wonders of the World. For now, I will call it a day and let tomorrow's new and fascinating things excite me. I do wonder.

CAVES

How many of you have a cave in your backyard or somewhere near your house? Unless you live in the country where a mountain range is available and caves are plentiful, not many of you can say yes. In my opinion, everyone lives in a cave but I call them houses. If you think about it we tunnel inside our house when it gets dark ... well, maybe some of us ... and we use electricity instead of a stick fire for lighting or warmth. We close our doors and lock them to provide safety. Cavemen might have piled brush near and around a cave opening to thwart impending doom of pre-historic animals stalking them to have a good meal. We have beds to cozy our bodies. Cave dwellers perhaps used anything available, such as branches or skins of animals to stave off cold.

When I was a little girl, we would go to Devil's Den State Park to "maybe" walk through caves. The "maybe" turned into gasps as Mother was claustrophobic and figured if she had the phobia, we all did. Our venture took us up 59 Highway and then we turned off onto Highway 220 north of Cedarville. The road was seldom graded and could be treacherous if the car broke down or you had a flat tire. Various parts of the steep inclined road made for some "close your eyes and hit the floorboard moments." Houses were far apart and shotguns were plentiful, especially by those not eager to have someone trespass on their property. If you were lucky to find a living person willing to help, you might be able to get to your destination.

You best be watching for Cujo, the Saint Bernard, a pack of German Shepherds named Jaws, Bear Trap or Sic'em, or Lock Jaw the Pit Bull. People had dogs, not pets, and if you looked at them sideways, you might not live through the day. Being stuck out in the boonies was not something I enjoyed but Daddy always carried a 45 caliber pistol and Mother toted a 38 revolver, so safety wasn't an issue. Daddy had enough ammo in the car to blow everything to kingdom come. Although I didn't know it at the time, he had spark plugs, spare water for the radiator, gasoline in a glass jug, a siphon tube, plenty of fan belts and radiator hoses and itchy wool army blankets anchored in the trunk.

Daddy wanted to show us what the CCC (Civilian Conservations Corps) built during the 1930's when the area was set aside as a park. Massive stones were nestled in and around and used as supports for cabin structures. The native stone sustaining the Lee Creek dam was built by the hands of the CCC. All of this great park's construction was part of F.D Roosevelt's New Deal. It was and still is a natural wonder of the state of Arkansas. It provides captivating moments for travelers and to all of us who live in the Natural State.

Guess what! Devil's Den was not the only area having caves for this exploring kid. Right here in Van Buren, hidden in the bluffs overlooking the Arkansas River and the Frisco railroad tracks, are caves. They may not tout winding, narrow, dank crevasses leading you to the opposite end of the cave but they are beautiful. Those caves were areas where hobos stayed after they hopped from a train's box car.

SKIPPING DOWN MEMORY LANE

In fact, if you travel Arkansas Street on a regular basis, you pass a cave every day. You didn't know it, did you? The cave was part of my stomping grounds. There weren't many large trees as there is today and a portion of the cave could be seen from the street. The boulders, surrounding the area, were a great place to stand upon and view the panoramic span toward downtown Van Buren.

A bunch of us kids would traipse up the dusty road of Arkansas Street to enjoy the cool atmosphere of the cave. It was large or maybe it seemed large as I was so small. We would take a picnic lunch, a few raw potatoes and wire clothes hangers. There were plenty of dry sticks to make a fire but we learned in a hurry not to build the fire so far back in the cave. Smoke would choke you to death as it billowed toward the cave opening. We would gasp for breath as our lungs filled with putrid smoke and then we ran like the devil to get fresh air. We knew peanut butter and jelly sandwiches wouldn't last long, so using wire clothes hangers; we skewered potatoes to roast on the fire. The outside of the potato would char while the metal hanger blistered its interior. I think we must have invented the Hot Potato game because it became a tossing game to see who could hold it the longest. Most times the potato was slung to the dirt floor or flung on the rocks.

Each time I go up Arkansas Street I peer upward to the elusive cave now hidden by many years' growth of saplings, poison ivy and scrub brush. The boulder we once stood upon isn't there and I am sure the paths we carved succumbed to erosion. I wonder if our old campfire sticks inside the cave lay undisturbed and if the mounds of half eaten charred potatoes have fossilized. I guess it's a part of life that I don't know the answers to these questions ... it would take the fun out of remembering the cave and our escapades. The next time I pass you on Arkansas Street, I will be careful to watch you as you look for the cave!

P.S. Heed this warning, before you traipse up the cliffs to look for the caves make sure you have permission as it may be private property. Take note for copperheads as they are plentiful.

MONKEY SEE, MONKEY DO

By now, having read my stories, you know I grew up on Henry Street. You also know my father's mother, my grandmother Brannam, lived two houses north of me. I loved going to Grandma's house … that is, when I could sneak off from my eagle eyed sister or Mother. Sometimes, though, if I unlatched the gate in a furtive way, neither one of them would know I was missing. Actually, I was not missing; I knew where I was at all times. Problem was, I didn't want someone telling me what, when, where or how to do something.

The blasted gate was a thorn in my side, sort of like a flea on an itchy dog. To hear my sister yell at me when I sneaked off was like listening to a foghorn. In the hollers, any type of yell carried for miles and because of it, the neighbors knew I was on the lam. Why heck, all I wanted to do was go to Grandma's house but pointing fingers gave away my intended target.

Getting into Grandma's yard was another thing I had to do without detection. I had to be as quiet as a mouse, on tippy toes and then I had to pray for Divine intervention. I was on alert the minute my feet hit the corner of her lot and my eyes scanned every square inch. Unfortunately, I had no idea where the famous nefarious nemesis would be lurking. Most critters and I get along, sans a few I would rather not come in contact with and Grandma's, Poncho, was one of them.

Poncho was not an ordinary critter and it certainly didn't walk on four feet. No, this critter had two feet and could fly faster than a speeding bullet.

Where Grandma got him, I have no idea but I told her, in one of my screaming fits, she needed to take him back from whence he came. Her reply to me was that he was protecting his domain and he wouldn't hurt a fly. Horsefeathers ... duh, goose feathers! Poncho was a danged old goose, one that I wished was fricasseed on a spit or tarred and feathered and run out on a rail. He was gray and white with a bit of black on his wings and as mean and wicked as the fiery furnace of hell. This goose should never have hatched. Whatever Grandma fed him had to be nasty as his temperament was that of the devil.

You couldn't ignore him as he was king of the lot. If he had been a dog, no eye contact or touch would have worked. Poncho was evil and sneaky. He would hide under porch steps, behind trees or anything that could disguise his ornery, tough old hide. He was almost invisible until he caught sight of me and then the race began. I could run fairly fast but his webbed feet could beat me to the finish line. If his feet didn't keep pace, his wings took flight. I was outnumbered four to two in that his wings and feet lambasted me with all their might. Poncho would lower his head almost to the ground with his long skinny neck hunched in an "I'm gonna bite you" mode.

Bite is not the word for it! That stupid goose, in an all out lunge, gripped my rear end and legs with a powerful clamp. It felt like my skin was in a vise with nowhere to go. He wouldn't turn loose and then if he accidently did, he took another chunk out of my rear, legs or arms. My skin was black and blue from the incessant pinches from his beak and I got tired of it. The only way to make him turn loose was to grab his neck and squeeze until he couldn't breathe. It was a standoff with me squeezing his neck and him drawing blood. I hated that goose but it was reciprocal ... he hated me. I didn't scratch his back with reciprocity. I threatened to wring his bloody neck, throw him over my shoulder, haul him home and let Mother bake him.

Poncho was not the only bad tempered critter on her lot. I do believe when they handed out critters to Grandma, she gave them lessons in how to be bad. Sometimes Grandma's temper would shame hell and make you beg for cold water. How she could be so cantankerous and have those critters be putty in her hands is anyone's guess. Where Poncho roamed there was no fence as whenever he took a notion to fly, he did. However, on the lower portion of her property (two lots), a fence was erected. It wasn't an ordinary chicken wire fence; it was a sharp barbed wire confinement. If you dared go inside without a cousin or Grandma, you took your life into realms of idiocy. Inside the fence was a stupid, and I do mean stupid, braying donkey. He was chocolate brown with ears the size of sabers. His teeth and breath was disgusting. It made me gag. When he was angry his ears clung to the side of his head, his four feet plowed the ground and whammo, his rear feet kicked backward. Heaven help the poor soul standing behind him because he could cold cock you and your lights would be out for days.

On rare occasions, my cousins, my sister, Hazel, and I would try to ride this loco donkey. I think Grandma must have fed him rotten hay or moonshine to make him so nuts. The only nutty and loco people were us as our brains turned to mush. Grandma would yell, "Monkey see, monkey do." One person would hold a leather rein while the brave soul without any brains, hopped on his back. Even though he had on blinders I do believe he could see behind his head. The minute someone took hold of the reins an all out war raged. We landed on our backsides so many times we appeared to have our rears in front of us. When he couldn't extract us in bucking format, he went straight for the barbed wire fence. If he couldn't kill us by bucking or stomping us into the ground, he found another way. The fence was his friend as he knew the barbs would do dastardly deeds to our bodies. Dastardly deeds, indeed! We wound up with gashes on our legs and clothing you couldn't mend.

Grandma had no need for a watch dog as she had a wild donkey wanting to kill wayward souls on the bottom half of her property and a goose at the front door eager to raise blood blisters. With all the mayhem and obstacles I encountered, I believe the only reason I went to Grandma's house was to hear her yell, "Monkey see, monkey do".

LYE SOAP

Talk about a stench! The aroma from making lye soap would blister the hairs out of the nose, curl up the toenails, take warts off the hands and make you sweat. It was grueling work but in order to have soap for bathing and laundry, the little woman (sometimes men) stood over a hot pot stirring the concoction till she / he was sun tanned.

Grandma used hog lard they rendered for this purpose. It might take a while to accumulate enough lard to make one batch of lye soap, because more often than not, the lard was used in cooking. Bacon grease was saved and added to the batch of collected lard. Rancid or not, the lard was used as nothing was thrown away. It didn't matter if it had an icky smell, lye soap wasn't edible and there was no lingering scent after you bathed. Fresh washed clothes hanging on a clothes line always smelled like spring sunshine and looked like white doves fluttering in the air. No yellow ocher tint remained on the clothes unless well water had an enormous amount of iron in the water. People in the country didn't have amenities we have today and utilized every ounce of "know how" to sustain family existence.

Grandma's big iron pot was used for making lye soap. It wasn't a pot to be moved from place to place as it was at least sixty inches in circumference, about two feet deep, over an inch thick with four small feet at its base and two handles at the top. It weighed as heavy as its appearance. To buy a can of lye wasn't necessary as the ashes from a fire place can be used as long as the ashes don't contain chunks of wood. In order to use it, water has to be poured over the ashes, left to stand for a period of time and drained. The ashy water is then substituted for a can of lye. I don't remember what proportions she used as it was poisonous and irritating to the skin, eyes, nose and throat. She wouldn't let me near it.

The old black pot was in an area cleared for making soap. Piling chunks of wood around its perimeter, the pot took on an eerie glow as the incinerate heat cranked out billowing smoke. The massive chunks of lard melted in haste. Steam would rise from the pot as cool water was poured in a delicate stream into the center of the hot lard. When the oil and water began boiling, the cold, lye water she made from ashes was gently added. It might take thirty minutes to pour eight or sixteen ounces of lye water into the pot because it had to be done very slowly. Constant stirring with a large wooden stick was the name of the game. You couldn't let up or the lard and lye would congeal into blobs making the soap useless. It had to be smooth, like a fine silky hand lotion. For hours, we watched Grandma stir the cauldron making the lard, lye, and water to the right consistency. If need be, she would add more water. Somehow, she always knew when to stop the process. When the soap turned a delicate white shade, it was time to ladle the mixture into a boxes made specifically for bars of soap.

Cold water was poured on the embers under the iron pot and the ashes were left there to use for another batch of soap. When they cooled, Grandma would scoop them up, sift and lay aside until needed. Ladling took much care since the soap was scalding hot. Using heavy duty, homemade pot holders; she dipped a large enameled coffee pot into the soap and carried each load to the kitchen.

On the table, two boxes, approximately three feet long and a foot wide, had twelve, four inch sections neatly nailed in place to house the mixture. As if pouring a cup of coffee into a china cup, the soap flowed smoothly into each section. After the mixture sat for a couple of hours, she would use several strands of sewing threads and saw through the top layer to make uniformly straight bars. The excess, semi-hard slivers were laid aside to use as laundry soap, cleaning solutions or for washing the hair.

After twenty-four hours, a bar of soap could be used but it was normally too soft to last very long and melted under pressure. The actual cure for lye soap was about one week to make it last for several usages. The soap was used for a multitude of things, unlike our modern day products manufactured for specific household chores. Laundry, bathing, window washing, shampoo, disinfectant, flea killer (don't know if it worked), scrubbing floors to killing odors, one product ... lye soap ... did it all.

We've come a long way from a timeless era to one stop shopping but at what price? Could we digress to what our parents and grandparents did to preserve a part of our heritage? Making lye soap is only one thing they did but they did it well. If making lye soap is a forgotten part of our lives, what kind of legacy will we leave our children and grandchildren? Are we so dependent on someone else's resources; we don't make the time to do our own? Probably, but, if you don't mind ... I've had enough of black pots ... I'll buy a bar of lye soap!

GLOOM AND DOOM

This story has nothing to do with *Do You Remember*, my guest column in The Press Argus - Courier, but my personal take on today's economy. We live within our means; have a modest house and no large income. We have and always will work hard because it's how we were raised. The one thing I hate is gloom and doom but it seems to surround us everywhere we go. It's an insidious, mind altering, ego deflating pox, permeating souls and bodies to a stagnate standstill. It's in the paper, on television, massive re-runs of yesterday's news ... a constant, pound, pound, pound to the brain, until people hover in despair. Enough already!

We are, people, in a massive recession but we have been known, as a whole, to put up our dukes and fight ... fight like hell. Negativity breeds negativity and until we start to see a positive side in our mind set, we won't see an end to what ails us. The United States and world has been through this before and will again, no doubt, be in the same position several years down the road. Our boot straps are thick and our stamina is strong, so let's jerk them up to re-route us to positive thinking. Nowhere is it written, we have to suffer in silence or keep our mouths shut to appease elected officials. We are "THE PEOPLE" and we have freedom of speech.

No company should be "guaranteed" profits or should they dole out humongous bonuses to those corporate giants who hoard from the workers. After all, the workers are the ones who make things happen while the colossal sit on the golden throne amassing wealth. Until those "giants" are made to fork over money they think they earned and put it back in the economy, it will continue. No person, on this earth, is worth $54 million dollars because they are CEO. Titles are nothing more than titles, a brand of sorts, and are worth, maybe, the cost of a cup of coffee. Simply because a person has been dubbed "chief honcho" in charge of the bucket brigade doesn't mean he doesn't have to tote the bucket. They need to get off their duffs, pick up a shovel and gouge down in the dirt like all the other Americans. Their hands are dirty but not from doing peon work.

Some say bailing out banks (mortgage loans) and transportation (auto industry) has to be done to alleviate more people being laid off from jobs. Hello! Those "giants" whose greedy disposition put them in the eyes of bankruptcy should be willing to underwrite their failure with their own "pocket change." Will they do it? No way ... until, we, the people, start demanding them to do so. They are working with "our" money, saying, "Oh, woe is me." Do they go to bed at night worrying about where their next nickel will appear? No! Why not? Your nickel or your dollar/$$$ is in their pocket.

Every outsourcing company (moving jobs to foreign countries) should be made to pay a hefty tax (let's say ... $1 million per quarter) to maintain their "American" status in tax breaks. Pretty soon, the foreign soil won't look so appealing and they might wonder why sales have fallen. Could it be we won't buy their products? Sure, they say it costs less money to produce them overseas but if their revenue drops in loss of sales ... they have lost ... big time. Their wallets will soon be flattened like a pancake and they will be begging "we, the people" to embrace their stupidity. Bail out ... no way. They tell us to sink or swim, so by golly, if they want to survive, the life jackets need to be tossed our way. We are the buoyancy who keeps them afloat.

Millions of people have lost trillions of dollars through Wall Street. Life savings and retirements are squashed or erased because of speculative trading. We have no one to blame but ourselves and it's time to cut our losses and move forward. We can either wring our hands in despair or do like our parents and grandparents did during The Great Depression. We can make do with what we have, barter with other people in way of goods (trading something for something else) or SPEAK out.

Talking, in private, about what ails us won't do any good. You and I need to pick up pen and paper and write letters to our congressperson. If we don't see results from them ... then it's time to spark their attention by writing letters to the editors of newspapers. Don't stop with one newspaper or one letter. Inundate them with massive letter and telephone campaigns. One way or another, "WE the PEOPLE" can produce results. It's time to get angry, demand restitution from corporate greed and stop the madness. "Absolute power corrupts absolutely" and if we don't do something about it now, we will be among the corruptors.

TENT REVIVALS

It was hotter than blistering hell, the grass was as dead as dead could get and sitting inside a tent was not my cup of tea. Dust flew everywhere when kids shuffled their feet and tempers flared when sweat dripped down the brow. Those awful slats on folding wood chairs creaked and pinched skin if tilted in the wrong direction. The rules, according to parents, were to sit still and pay attention. It was impossible.

As a child, I never understood why a woman, dressed in her finest clothing or a man having the will to be garroted by a tie knotted at the throat would sit inside a tent during 100 degree weather. Heavy duty electric cords could be seen draping from the nearest utility pole lighting a 100 watt bulb in the center of the tent. Down the narrow pathway between rickety seats, a green carpeted grass (somewhat like those from funeral homes) tripped people as they began to sit at their chosen seat. If a hole was hidden under the fake grass you can bet your booties someone would splat forward. Somewhere along the way, a family of forty needed to plow over feet to get to their saved seats which happened to be next to the side of the tent. When it happened, patent leather shoes were scuffed beyond repair and big toes jammed into little toes. You couldn't walk, stand up straight or sit long enough to understand why the adults needed reviving. If adults were revived, I never saw it because all of us kids were exhausted to the max.

My earliest recollection of going to an old time tent revival (sans tent) it was somewhere close to Silver Bridge near Alma and situated on the north side of the two-way road. It was an all day event with a defining purpose but I was too young to understand the depth of its meaning. Early in the morning, the air was cool and crisp, tickling the nose with a faint scent of creek grasses while the creek water gave off its own aroma. Every sound and scent seemed magnified. Out in a wide open field cars lined up in rows and we waited for a signal to exit our cars. It was time for church service. Most people stood near or sat on the hood of their cars while the minister delivered his sermon. Some of the elderly sat inside the cars or were assisted closer to hear the minister. A cow or two in the distance competed with their own delivery. So help me, on this day in history, inside or outside the cars, we were chewed alive by mosquitoes. Being close to the creek, the mosquitoes thrived and swarmed by millions eager to take a chunk out of bare skin. The adults tolerated the inconvenience while I swatted them.

Then, after the service, somewhere around noon, the women of the church laid quilts on the ground. Food of all kinds came from the trunks and back seats of cars. It was a feast to behold. Fried chicken, potato salad, homemade rolls, and cakes and pies filled almost every square inch of the quilts. If anyone went away hungry, it was their own fault. Around four in the afternoon, when everyone finished "grazing" and having a good old confab, the core of the agenda began. The young children snapped to attention when we were told to gather with their parents. It meant we needed to watch and listen to divine intervention by immersion. Heck, I didn't even know what it meant but found out in short order. It was baptism by a good old fashion dunking in the creek. I don't know how many people stood at the edge of the creek but there were many ... both young and old.

One by one, they inched near water. While the minister held their hands, they prayed together. I watched as each person, fully clothed in their best frocks and suits, disappeared beneath the water. The congregation and minister prayed as the minutes ticked away. It seemed an eon before each individual surfaced and I wondered if any of them would die from water in their lungs or from a snake bite. I held my breath and shook with Goosebumps even though the temperature was reaching double digits.

I was relieved this part was over but it didn't end there. It was beginning to get dark. Clothes on those baptized were dry and the quilts no longer lay on the ground. Empty food containers went inside car trunks. Although there was no tent or electricity to light the way, kerosene lamps dotted the field in droves. The flickering light and smelly undertones of kerosene sent me reeling to the back seat of the car. I was ready to go home, sick to my stomach and unable to keep my eyes open.

A thunderous roar jolted me awake. My eyes wouldn't stay shut even with modern day superglue. I expected to peek out the window and see a warpath of Indians circling the encampment. It was not Indians but the sound of Amen, Halleluiah and Praise the Lord. It got louder and louder. People were coming unhinged with inner excitability in being revived.

SKIPPING DOWN MEMORY LANE

This event was a prelude to actual tent revivals we attended. Some were held on the grounds where Consolidated Printed is located and others at Blakemore Field. On occasion, a tent would pop up at the top of Log Town Hill and in a field near old 64-71 highway across from Gracelawn Cemetery. It didn't matter if it was hot or cold outside; we went to those tent revivals and sometimes a rambunctious boy sat off consecutive blasts of "collected" firecrackers. It made adults bounce off the tent and revived them in a hurry.

Indoor baptismal areas and air-conditioning put a near halt to old timey tent revivals. The one thing those two things could not change was this wide eyed little girl and her impression of the masses being revived in a cow pasture.

MOTHER'S DAY – RED OR WHITE

Have you ever noticed the timing of blooming roses? Generally, they begin their first bud in April and continue blossoming until the last rose of summer fades into the sunset. Grandma Brannam had the most exquisite white climber and right before Mother's Day, it sprang forth with generous, tight, up-right buds. Its sweet aroma cascaded downward from the trellis but we weren't allowed to pick any of the beauty springing forth. There was a reason but as a child I couldn't fathom the caution. My eager hands wanted to pluck the delicate beauties to smother my body with their perfume. It didn't happen as those first roses were set aside to commemorate deceased mothers. The word deceased was not in my vocabulary but it soon became my introduction to Mother's Day, a fine lesson never to be forgotten.

Being so small and pinned with a red rose for Sunday church service, I felt special until all the other children showed up with a straight pinned rose. It was a letdown knowing they were horning in on my "special effects" day. Like me, they didn't comprehend the magnitude of Mother's Day but did get the jolt of being pricked by a crooked pin.

I didn't know why this day was sobering but along with my family, donned with red roses from Mother's rose bush, we smelled wonderful. Looking around the church pews, white roses adorned many of the elderly and a tear could be seen as it bolted from the eyes. I wondered why they were so sad and got the courage to ask the question burning a hole in my mind.

Turning around in my pew, I asked Mrs. Garland Sagely why she was wearing a white rose and told her I would trade my red rose for her white one because the white rose smelled best. She told me the white rose was sweeter because of her memories. Mother gasped at my cheekiness. At the time, I don't remember if I understood the answer but I do recall being jerked up by my armpits and traveling down the aisle to the front stoop. Daddy told me not to be asking such impertinent questions and to keep my face centered on the preacher because I would learn a good lesson.

As it was in those days, you were supposed to keep your mouth shut ... seen and not heard. Those words and actions didn't hold well with me. I was vocal and wasn't about to shove myself in a corner until I found out why everyone was so bleary eyed, red faced and snotty nosed. Never in my life did I see so many ladies curlicue embroidered hankies and men's handkerchiefs dabbing at eyes than I did in that single church service. It was a sight to behold. Why on earth didn't they be frank and say, "Look, kid, you wear a red rose because your mother is alive. Be thankful and shout it to the ends of the earth."

If I had gotten any closer to Daddy, I would have been on the other side of him. I was nodding off and wedged under his massive arms. Apparently, in such close proximity, he was uncomfortable being pushed against the end of the pew. In order for him to help pass the collection plates, my limp body was passed over to Mother. When I woke up, I was curled up in

Mother's lap and she was caressing my hair. It was at that moment, looking up at her and seeing her big brown eyes, when Mother's Day and the thoughts of my mother connected.

It was an epiphany of gigantic proportions hearing Mrs. Sagely's sage comments and the pastor's words about the blood of the lamb. I remember whispering, "I love you, Mother. It's your day, isn't it?" I can still feel the tear as it fell from her eye and landed on my cheek. It was warm and impacting and her words carved into my mind. "Yes, it's my day and one day you will understand." Mother was my perfect red rose, unblemished, sweet, guiding, loving, giving and protective. It was her thorns of protection keeping me in check.

Oh, how I do understand. Being a mother is one of the most rewarding things I have ever done in my life. My children have been my greatest achievement and a blessing. They are my sweet, delightful rosebuds having come to life spreading their petals to fruition. Nothing can compare to being a mother except for the rose.

The rose can stand the test of time with storms, high winds and predators, as does a mother, in guarding her fine buds. Protected by prickly thorns, the buds know they can curl themselves under a limb and be shielded from harm's way. As a mother is powerful by nourishing a child, the rose feeds too. By its delectable aroma and sweet unfurling petals, it draws and captures the hearts of many. A mother's heart is open as she unfurls her arms to her children.

I know why Grandma Brannam kept me from picking the roses. It wasn't because she didn't want me to have the flowers. It was because the first white rose for Mother's Day was set aside for special memories about her mother. As a grandmother, she was protecting me from the formidable thorns.

The red rose, with its deep red veins, is a symbol to proclaim and rejoice living and the white rose, void of pigment in its petals, evokes deep and powerful memories of those gone to their rewards.

Today, I would give the world to wear a red rose and watch my mother pin the flower to my dress but I can't. What I can remember and hold dear is the memory of a tear falling to my cheek and telling Mother I loved her. A rose can be a rose by any name but my beautiful rose, Anna Lucille Hawkins Brannam, was called Mother.

If you wear a red rose, rejoice. If you wear white, we will shed tears together. Happy Mother's Day.

FOUR-WAY TEST

When I received an email from Tom and Sue Moore on January 15 requesting I speak at the Van Buren Rotary Club, I felt honored. At the same time, I wondered how on earth I would incorporate storytelling and my love for writing with the club's activities. How would two separate entities mesh together? Since I have no problem talking, I agreed to be the guest speaker. On January 21, I walked into the Van Buren Community Center, unprepared for the speech. I had no notes. I figured if I couldn't talk off the cuff, I didn't need to be there. The only problem is that I can't say anything less than one hour. Twenty minutes to talk is like taking a deep breath. I would adhere to my time frame because there were those needing to get back to work.

As I opened the foyer door, aromas of food flitted through the air. It was a classic memory, as aromas take us back in time to help set the stage. Signing the guest book, I glanced around the small room. Several people had gathered, selecting, I assumed, their favorite seats. It was another way I use to remember seating arrangements at various functions and church. Most often, everybody can remember who sat where and if the chair or pew is vacant, the void is prominent. It's another page of memories.

My eye connected to Judge Floyd "Pete" Rogers, my friend for many years. A big smile popped across his face, a smile I could never forget. We sang together at church and his antics, during choir practice, left us all in stitches. Pulling out a chair next to him, I sat down asking how he was doing. His beloved wife, Hazel, was no longer on this earth but he was coping. He was doing farm work, puttering around and enjoying his children. He was still connected to her as he drove her Cadillac to the meeting. Trucks are his forte but this car was special. I understood. As he ate, I filled my plate and joined him. He questioned the small portion telling me it wouldn't keep a bird alive. My response was I didn't want green stuff sticking out of my teeth when I spoke. His cell phone rang, there was a small conversation and he asked me if I knew how to turn it off. I told him I didn't know but stomping it on the ground might work. He didn't take my advice.

The room was filling to capacity. One by one, several people I knew walked into the room. Some faces were familiar but I didn't know their names. I never forget a face even if we have never been introduced. They filled lunch plates and proceeded with the meeting. Since I had never been to a Rotary Club meeting, I didn't know what to expect. It was laid back and jovial but with a distinct meaning. I was impressed as The Pledge of Allegiance laid the foundation to its beginning. Rotary rituals ensued but I had no clue what they meant. As long as they knew what they were doing, it was okay with me. Waiva Strain, the piano player, was not there so we sang; *It's a Grand Old Flag*, a cappella.

It was my time to speak. Telling them my love for writing and doing the Press Argus - Courier stories was not a job, it was a privilege and pleasure. I gave a small introduction about myself, where I grew up in the hollers and how it was considered the wrong side of the tracks. If it was, I didn't know it as everyone lived on either side of the tracks. It was the "connotation" of tracks and unattractive vibes. I was perceived as a child ... stubborn, opinionated, mouthy and defiant.

The Rotary Club Four-Way Test, I pointed out, is somewhat like my writing techniques. 1. Is it the TRUTH? 2. Is it FAIR to all concerned? 3. Will it build GOODWILL and BETTER FRIENDSHIPS? 4. Will it be BENEFICIAL to all concerned?

Like the Rotary Club, where they hinge their humanitarian efforts on these four tests, writing has to have a modicum of these virtues. Truth ... even though fiction writing is not truth, its poetic license. Fair ... yes, as people have options to their choice of reading materials. Goodwill and better friendships ... absolutely, as I have met many wonderful people and heard their stories. Beneficial ... without question, as many people have begun to know the importance of writing down what they have done, where it happened and what they remember as a child. If not, your memories are moot and you won't leave a footprint. Only rocks live forever and they won't tell your stories.

As I told them, you can't live in the future without having lived in the past. When a person is born, they are automatically a part of the past. It's what you do with the past that will push you into the future. People are like traffic signs. Some are stuck at a stop sign afraid to go forward. Others yield to avoid failure. Some move cautiously at amber lights, hesitating until someone tells them it's safe. Since I am a positive person, a green light is my destination.

It's my opinion, The Rotary Club moves on green lights. This group of fine women and gentlemen has done many generous, beneficial, and worthwhile humanitarian deeds for the City of Van Buren and its citizens. RI (Rotary International) President-elect Ray Klinginsmith says it best. "The words I have selected to describe Rotary's current mission and to highlight our achievements are what we do best: Building Communities -- Bridging Continents."

The Van Buren Rotary Club: 2450, District 6110 was founded in 1920. If you are interested in becoming a Rotary Club Member, they meet every Thursday at noon in the Van Buren Community Center, 224 South 11th Street in Van Buren. Check out their blog: http://vanburenrotary.blogspot.com/

BROWNIES

If you look real hard, I bet you can find a Brownie hidden somewhere in an attic, cedar chest or old barn. I'm not talking about chocolate but cameras. We have come a long way since the first inexpensive Brownie was put on the market. Eastman Kodak made the popular camera in 1900. It was a simple brown cardboard box but the Brownie could capture two and one-fourth inch pictures.

However, in 1814, pictures were being captured from the same type of box. The photo, taken in Paris by Nicéphore Niépce, used a similar box camera made by Charles and Vincent Chevalier. Guess what? Cameras have been around since camera obscura (means dark room in Latin). It was invented by Abu Ali Al-Hasan Ibn al-Haitham who was born in Basra in 965-1039 AB. It was used as an optical device. This type of camera projects surrounding images on a screen. Even farther back, in 470 BC to 390 BC, the pinhole camera was devised by Mo-Ti. He was a Chinese philosopher and founder of Mohism. A pinhole camera was used by Aristotle as he understood the optical principle. It's the same type of "camera" we use today as we watch a solar eclipse. All of us know that looking directly toward the sun during a solar eclipse, blindness can occur. Our "camera" is made of two pieces of paper. One has a tiny pin hole and the other captures the image. In this instance, with our back to the sun, the sun's image shines through the pin hole to the piece of blank paper.

There have been many ways to develop film. People, using the daguerreotype in 1829, captured images on silver-plated copper by placing iodine on the silver. By dipping the image in silver chloride pictures emerged. Then there was negative to positive images from Henry Fox Talbot, who named his form of film, calotype. Talbot was a contemporary to Daguerre who invented the daguerreotype.

There have been tintypes, wet plate and dry plate negatives all before Eastman Kodak who called his the flexible roll film. From there, in 1935, came Kodachrome. By the 1940's color was used in all film markets. We went from all of these to the Polaroid, called the Land Camera. Edwin Land, founder of the Polaroid Corporation, introduced his first commercial self developing camera in 1947.

Most everyone had a Brownie camera and enjoyed snapping pictures. Those are the pictures we think of when we go through old family albums. Each tells a story and brings back memories. A lot of people, including me, bought the film, snapped the pictures and then could not afford to have them developed. Rolls of undeveloped film lay in drawers or some obscure place waiting to be exposed. I don't know why it seemed so inconvenient to walk to the drug store to drop off the film so we could enjoy the pictures. The drug store was usually the place where everyone went to take the film. There was no instant developing service and it would take several weeks to retrieve the pictures. Was it actually because the money was not there or were we too nonchalant about the whole process? Whatever the decision, we chose what we chose to do. After my parents passed away, I found several rolls of undeveloped Brownie film. What was on those precious rolls and would they unhinge their secrets of the past?

Those rolls of film were a treasure trove. One very old roll of film was black and white and the later variety was color. Some were of Daddy when he worked at the smelter. His clothes were black with soot and he looked tired. A few included Daddy holding a favorite pistol as he stood beside an old car. He was in his element with guns and cars and the smile on his face revealed pleasure. Mother appeared to be chasing a rooster in one of the pictures ... probably because it spurred her with its talon. Maybe she was going to boil its tough old hide to get revenge or perhaps she was trying to ignore it. It's hard to tell what was happening. Mother was svelte and beautiful as her housedress seemed to flip in the picture with the movement of her body. Daddy was tall, handsome and thin as a rail. Age had not crept into their lives and everything around them stood still with time. My aunt and uncle were in two of the pictures guzzling down bottles of spirits. They were a young happy-go-lucky couple caught in time and place in their lives.

These old photos were worth their weight in gold and I could only imagine color. The newer color roll had Mother and Daddy in their later years. Mother wore a pink hat and matching clothes. Daddy was in a brown suit. The car they stood beside was new. The remaining pictures were those of their vacation. The difference of the black and white to color pictures was astounding. Time told it all. Not all of the pictures developed and it made me wonder what was on them. What were their secrets?

SKIPPING DOWN MEMORY LANE

We are in an age of zoom lens, downloadable pictures with what the new and exciting world offers. Yet, the simple Brownie camera with no bells or whistles unleashed, for me, the mother lode of its undeveloped film. Something so old, forgotten for whatever reason and laying dormant inside a junk drawer for many years ... came alive and zinged my heart.

EPILOGUE

Now that you have read these stories I hope you will be eager to read the trilogy. Each story I pen fills me with happiness and sends me to heights of nostalgic remembrances never to be repeated. What used to be is no longer. Times have changed, eras have passed and things have advanced but one thing is forever etched while we are living. No technological devices can change the pictures in our mind as we reflect on our memories.

Made in the USA
Charleston, SC
12 January 2012